CONTENTS

GAUDÍ
BUILDER OF VISIONS

720·92
01374

Philippe Thiébaut

Antoni Gaudí i Cornet was born on 25 June 1852 in Reus, in the province of Tarragona. His whole career was closely linked with another city: Barcelona, capital of Catalonia. Here, between 1883 and 7 June 1926 (the day on which he was knocked down by a tram), he created almost all his works. These include private residences, schools, apartment blocks, a park and, most famously, a cathedral—the Templo Expiatorio de la Sagrada Familia—on which he worked from 1883 until his death, when the building was left unfinished.

CHAPTER 1

THE ARCHITECT AND THE CITY

Right: Gaudí in about 1878, at the time he was finishing his studies and starting to work on the urban decoration of Barcelona. Left: the triumphal arch designed by Josep Vilaseca for the Universal Exhibition, which opened in Barcelona in 1888.

The beginning of Gaudí's career coincided with preparations for the Barcelona Universal Exhibition of 1888, an event that symbolized the prosperity of the city and confirmed the success of its middle classes. In spite of the stock market crash of 1882, of considerable social instability and of intense anarchist activity, the city was experiencing a period of quite exceptional political, economic, and cultural energy. Thanks to the relationship that they maintained with Spain's American colonies (which were to be lost in 1898), the progress that they encouraged in agriculture, and their investment in industrial development, Barcelona's middle classes were becoming ever wealthier.

Not only was the city's port one of the largest transit points for freight on the shores of the Mediterranean, but also its blast furnaces made it the undisputed industrial capital of Spain.

On 20 May 1888, the day of the official opening of the Universal Exhibition by María Cristina, the regent, a salvo of 432 cannon shots was let off by the international fleet anchored in Barcelona's harbor (below). The intense activity at the harbor seemed to contradict a statement frequently made at the time, that Barcelona lived with its back to the sea.

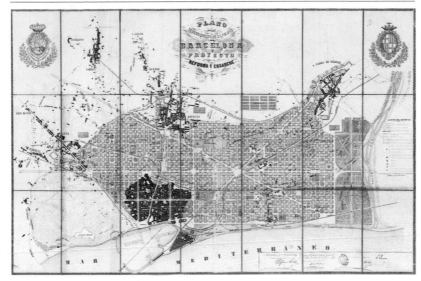

An expanding city

This rapid development led to a significant increase in the population, which rose from 350,000 in 1878 to 509,000 in 1897, reaching 587,000 in 1910. This enlarged population was accommodated with no difficulty at all, because the city had also grown considerably, its expansion made possible by the demolition of the Ciutadella, the old military fortification, which had begun in 1854. Built according to the plan for gridlike expansion drawn up by engineer and town planner Ildefons Cerdà i Sunier (1816–75), a new city came into being: this was the Eixample (Extension). Projecting beyond the city walls, it developed in the rational but monotonous form of a checkerboard, running alongside the medieval city from Plaça de Catalunya (Catalonia Square) to the little village of Gràcia. This huge grid took some time to fill, and at the end of the 1870s the city still gave the impression of a vast, empty space. However, the Eixample gradually became urbanized by the bustle of the 1880s, which was stimulated by preparations for the Universal Exhibition.

In 1851 the Barcelona city council requested the permission of the Spanish state to demolish the city's fortifications. Eight years later, Ildefons Cerdà i Sunier was engaged by royal decree to draw up a plan for its expansion. This led to strong protests and demands for Catalan autonomy, which forced the City Hall to organize a competition. The idea was accepted by Madrid, but on condition that consultation take place and that the winning plans be compared with Cerdà's scheme. The winner was the municipal architect, but Cerdà's plan (above) had already been approved and was accepted in 1860.

Catalan identity

The combination of major demographic expansion and rapid economic development created highly favorable conditions for the flowerng of intellectual and cultural life. The latter's main thrust was the reestablishment of Catalonia's identity, which had suffered greatly from political centralization (focused on Madrid), and from the supremacy of Castilian as the administrative language. During the Romantic period, the Renaixença (Renaissance) movement had stimulated a revival of interest in the language and traditions of Catalonia. It was not until the end of the 19th century, however, that this tendency, backed up by the power of Barcelona, produced concrete results. One notable development was the launch of the magazine *L'Avenç* (Progress), the first issue of which appeared in 1881, providing the movement with a means to publicize itself. *L'Avenç* was created by the initiative of Jaume Massó i Torrents, who also made the first attempt to establish a Catalan grammar. Although *L'Avenç* played only a very limited role in the artistic sphere, it spurred the intellectual elite to embrace Catalan culture and

become involved in Modernism, the term that was used to denote Catalonia's particular style of Art Nouveau.

Barcelona: the Modernist city

The impetus given by the Universal Exhibition, together with the artistic climate of the late 19th century, made Barcelona architecturally one of the most exciting cities in Europe. Among the leading exponents of Modernism were Josep Vilaseca i Casanovas (1848–1910), Lluís Domènech i Montaner (1849–1923), whose most outstanding work is the Palau de la Música (1905–8); Joseph Puig i Cadafalch (1867–1956); and Josep Maria Jujol. Polychromy and ornamentation, eclecticism, a more or less strong engagement with the Gothic style and a sculptural, sometimes organic handling of surfaces characterized Modernism.

For the Universal Exhibition, temporary buildings were raised alongside others that were intended to be

The Passeig de Gràcia (left) is one of the two avenues about 22 yards (20 meters) wide that diagonally bisect the vast grid of streets laid out by Cerdà in 1859. Over the following decades, enormous amounts of capital were invested in developing the center of the Eixample. The shops, restaurants, and theaters that were installed there attracted a crowd. This was admirably described by Narcís Oller, master of Catalan naturalism, in his novel *La Febre d'or* (Gold Fever) of 1890–92.

The quantity of materials used on the buildings for the Universal Exhibition was such that the following report appeared in the columns of a daily newspaper at the time: "The output from all our brick factories is almost exhausted; the same is true of cement, which is arriving in great quantities from various parts of the principality and from abroad. For the Great Palace of Industry alone, 800 hundred-weight of this material are being used every day." Lower left, the Palace of Industry in the course of its construction.

The construction of the polychrome triumphal arch at the entrance to the Universal Exhibition (left) was the high point in the career of architect Josep Vilaseca i Casanovas, who was very active in the 1880s. Vilaseca was an interesting figure in the artistic life of Barcelona in the last two decades of the 19th century. As a teacher at the Provincial School of Architecture, he considerably broadened the cultural horizons of the students there. He was particularly concerned with the relationship between architecture and the decorative arts. In 1883–35 he designed a Japanese-style facade for an umbrella shop on the Plaça de la Boquería. This was unique in Barcelona's urban décor. The house that he built in 1884 for Francesc Vidal's cabinetmaking workshops may be seen as a symbol of the renaissance of the decorative arts in Barcelona. It was also in this small neo-Gothic building that the furniture, which Gaudí designed for the Palau Güell, was made.

permanent. Among the buildings that still stand today are two that give an idea of the exhibition's architectural bias: one is the triumphal arch that Josep Vilaseca built as the entrance to the exhibition; the other is the Castell des Tres Dragons (Three Dragons Castle), a café-restaurant that now houses the Museu de Zoologia (Zoological Museum), designed by Domènech i Montaner, also the architect of the Hotel Internacional, which was demolished after the exhibition. Whereas Vilaseca's triumphal arch is a decidedly unorthodox reinterpretation of the classical model, the castle re-creates the image of the idealized medieval castle, albeit with the benefit of modern industrial techniques: its

facades are held up by a structure made of laminated iron. A feature that the two buildings have in common is the fact that both are constructed almost entirely in red engineering brick, an old and relatively inexpensive material whose virtues had been praised in books about architecture since the end of the 1860s. The spaces between them are so slight that the bricks look as if they have been laid without cement. This was made possible by the ever-increasing standardization of bricks, which not only meant that they had perfectly accurate dimensions but also that they could be laid quickly and easily. The walls and facings form a continuous surface that is broken only when a deliberate decision has been made

Lluís Domènech i Montaner, a politician, was also an architect who left a profound mark on the urban landscape of Barcelona. As well as the Castell des Tres Dragons (above), he designed the Hospital de Sant Pau (1902–12), the Palau de la Música (1905–8), and private residences, including the Casa Lléo Morera.

to vary architectural outlines or add ornamentation. Clearly Catalan architects were well informed about new building techniques, and were anxious fully to exploit their advantages.

Gaudí: formation and early years

In a climate of vitality and cultural resurgence, Gaudí was thus but one of a whole group of highly talented and innovative architects, albeit the most original and inventive of them. Having begun his career as a draftsman, he was to remain closely concerned with the practical aspects of architecture, being involved in the smallest detail and personally solving problems on site as they arose. He also read assiduously, not only the writings of Viollet-le-Duc (1814–79), whose analytical and rationalist approach to the Gothic style exerted a strong influence on young architects of the late 19th to the early 20th centuries, but also those of the authors of the Renaixença and writings on philosophy and aesthetics. Through field trips he became familiar with Catalan medieval architecture. This gave him a strong feeling for his native region. He also upheld Christian ethics and looked to nature as a source of inspiration. Gaudí did not participate in the 1888 Universal Exhibition. By that time he had, however, already contributed to the embellishment of Barcelona. Although his scheme of 1877 for a monumental fountain in the Plaça de Catalunya had not been accepted, the imposing stone and bronze lampposts that he designed the following year for a competition organized by the city of

One of Gaudí's first projects for street furniture was the design of a public lavatory. For this, the young architect was commissioned by Enrique Girossi, a businessman who had sought permission from Barcelona's city council to install and manage about 15 public conveniences that were to be located at various points in the city. Gaudí's design (above) was rejected by Girossi and was never realized. This was not the case with the various designs for lampposts, including those on the Plaça Reial (right), that Gaudí had produced at the same period.

Barcelona were erected on the Plaça Reial, which was officially opened in September 1879, and also on the Pla de Palau. After this the theme of urban lighting was taken further, providing Modernist Barcelona with some astonishing creations. In 1888, for instance, Pere Falqués i Urpí (1850–1916) designed two sets of gigantic and exuberant metal streetlights, one set of which shows the influence of Gaudí.

Gaudí's lampposts date from the time that he began to work with architect Josep Fontseré i Mestres (1829–97), project manager of the Parc de la Ciutadella, whose remodeling after the destruction of the 18th-century citadel was part of the building program for the Universal Exhibition. Gaudí worked for Fontseré from 1877 to 1882, and he clearly played an important part in the design of the gate, the trophies, and the wrought-iron lampposts at the entrance to the park.

A classical training

Gaudí went to work for Fontseré one year before receiving his architect's diploma on 15 March 1878. He had received his high school education from the fathers of the Escuelas Pias in Reus, his native town, and moved to Barcelona in 1869 to study

architecture but was not admitted to the Provincial
School of Architecture until 1873, when he was 22 years
old. For this period, as indeed for the rest of his life,
the only documentation is in the form of accounts given
by his disciples, who collected the remarks that he
made: these are José F. Ràfols (*Gaudí*, 1929), César
Martinell (*Conversaciones con Gaudí*, 1952), Joan Bergós
(*Gaudí*, 1954) and Isidro Puig Boada (*El Pensamiento de
Gaudí*, 1981).

Joan Bergós relates that as a student Gaudí had
great difficulty in conforming to the rules of scholarly
exercises such as drafting plans. Among other stories,
Bergós told of how he had failed on a design for a
cemetery gate. Being unable to imagine the gate
separately from its surroundings, he started by drawing
the road leading to the cemetery, adding to it a hearse
and people in mourning, then a screen of cypress trees
and a sky full of gray clouds, so as to suggest an
atmosphere that was appropriate to the subject. The
tutor would not let Gaudí finish his drawing, explaining
that this was not the proper way to proceed. The young
man refused to correct what he had done, and left the
examination room. Gaudí also told his pupil about the
way in which he had passed the engineering test. He
had just gone to work for Fontseré, who at that time
was involved in creating the monumental fountain for
the Parc de la Ciutadella—which was inspired by the
fountain of the Palais Longchamp built in Marseilles by
Henry Espérandieu (1829–74). Gaudí had produced
brilliant static calculations to solve the tricky problem
of the tank controlling the flow of water. When his
engineering tutor, Joan Torras i Guardiola (1827–1910),
who was a friend of Fontseré, saw this project, he was
filled with admiration and asked who was responsible
for it. As a result he passed Gaudí on the day of the
examination even though the student knew absolutely
nothing about his course.

Now working as a draftsman in an agency, Gaudí
soon came in contact with professional architects and
real architectural issues. Before working for Fontseré,
he had been employed for two years by the diocesan
architect Francesc de Paula del Villar (1828–1903). Villar

In 1869 General Juan
Prim authorized the
demolition of the early
18th-century citadel. The
municipality decided to
turn the 150-odd acres
(60 hectares) of the site
into parks and gardens,
and in 1871 an inter-
national competition for
their design was declared.
The winner was the
architect Josep Fontseré i
Mestrès, whose plan,
accepted in 1872, was
greatly modified when
it was decided that
Barcelona should host the
1888 Universal Exhibition.

taught at the Provincial School of Architecture, whose principal was Elies Rogent i Amat (1821–97), a great admirer of the French "Diocesan School" and its rationalist tendencies. As principal, one of his first decisions was to make it compulsory to read the famous *Dictionnaire raisonné de l'architecture française du XIe au XVIe siècle* (Dictionary of French Architecture from the 11th to the 16th Centuries), published from 1854 to 1868 by Eugène Viollet-le-Duc.

As a teacher, Rogent devoted part of his course to the study of the theories of French architecture, and gave very particular emphasis to one key tenet: this was that the study of the architectural forms of the past did not indicate a backward-looking attitude but was the surest way to free oneself from the weight of the past by discovering the technical means by which solutions to

In the Parc de la Ciutadella Fontseré built imposing green-houses with an elegant chain of naves, and also a monumental fountain (above), which was completed in 1881. The fountain combined all the conventions of academicism and displayed an acute sense of theatricality. Fontseré is also known as the designer of El Born, the remarkable covered market that was built not far from the park between 1874 and 1876.

specific problems had been found. Statements made by Gaudí's disciples refer to the fact that their master regarded the discovery of French rationalism as having been fundamental to him during his years as a student.

This was despite the fact that Gaudí had been disappointed by Viollet-le-Duc's restoration of the Cathedral of Saint-Sernin in Toulouse, which he had visited during a trip to the southwest of France. He had also gone to Carcassonne, where Viollet-le-Duc had also worked. As he left, Gaudí is reported to have declared: "Let's go, we've learned nothing here. You have to study the Middle Ages to find out what they're all about. And carry on the Gothic style but at the same time save it from flamboyance." Nevertheless his admiration for Viollet-le-Duc's theoretical work led him to take a course of action that was to decide his future.

This opportunity was provided by the competition for the completion of Barcelona's medieval

cathedral, held in 1882. In the polemic that ensued, Gaudí sided with the supporters of the Modernist plan produced by the architect Joan Martorell i Montels (1833–1906)—not least because he himself, under Martorell's direction, had created the design for the façade that was presented for the competition—and opposed the proposal for a faithful reproduction of a 14th-century building.

The following year, Martorell was offered the job of chief architect of the projected Expiatory Temple of the Sagrada Familia. He turned it down, and put forward the name of Gaudí, who at the age of thirty-one embarked on the mission that was to occupy him for the rest of his life.

When Gaudí took control of the project for the Sagrada Familia in November 1883, following the resignation of Francesc de Paula del Villar, the neo-Gothic columns in the crypt (above), including the capitals, had already been erected. Gaudí carried them up higher, so that more light could come in. Above left: the elevation designed by Gaudí and presented by Martorell at the competition in 1882 for the completion of Barcelona Cathedral. Below: the elevation of the apse of the Cathedral of Saint-Sernin in Toulouse, as restored by Viollet-le-Duc.

Every architect working at the end of the 19th century, however much he wanted to shake off the yoke of styles inspired by the past, at some time in his career felt the irresistible pull of the historicist spirit of his time. Despite Gaudí's immense genius, he was no exception to this rule. He was also particularly influenced by Moorish architecture, which he regarded as showing a superior sense of technique.

CHAPTER 2

FROM EASTERN INFLUENCE TO CATALAN NATIONALISM

"Ornamentation has been and will be colored. Nature presents us with no object that is not colored; everything in vegetation, geology, topography and the animal kingdom is a more or less sharp contrast of colors. That is why every architectonic element must be colored."
Antoni Gaudí, 1878

Right: a detail of the cladding on the Casa Vicens. Left: a detail of the turret on the porter's lodge at the Finca Güell.

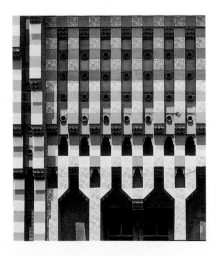

Gaudí had assiduously frequented the library at the Provincial School of Architecture in Barcelona, and as a result had a thorough knowledge of the history of architecture. The accounts of his disciples show how grateful he was to the medium of photography for providing very accurate images of buildings that had previously been reproduced only in engravings.

In relation to the study of the artistic forms and ornament of earlier times, every country selects areas that broadly correspond to the most glorious or emblematic periods of its national history. In the case of Spain there was a particular attraction to Mudéjar art, a Christian style blended with Moorish influences that flourished during the Reconquista of the 12th to the 15th centuries. Not only was the Mudéjar perceived as a highly successful formal synthesis; it was regarded as being at the very root of Spanish culture, and as a result it was placed at the vanguard in the struggle against a pervading eclecticism that was completely devoid of any historical basis.

"Spain has come to be represented, no one knows why, by Arabic architecture—that is to say, by the architecture of a conqueror under whose yoke she lived for a long time. No doubt the purpose is to make people want to come and visit the country. You must try to imagine the Alhambra Palace in Granada, in miniature it is true, but rejuvenated with all the splendors of fresh gilding, blue, red and green coloring, and skillfully restored arabesques…a facade that would be very good indeed if it were Spanish."

Curiosities of the Exhibition of 1878, Visitor's Guide

In 1859 José Amador de los Ríos delivered a lecture at the San Fernando Royal Academy of Fine Arts in Madrid entitled *El Estilo Mudéjar en Arquitectura* (The Mudéjar Style in Architecture). This gave rise to an often highly erudite debate that was reported in the periodicals of the time, and that led to the unanimous conclusion that it would not be possible to develop a modern national art without taking Mudéjar art into account. The intention to regenerate Spanish art on the basis of this source was pronounced loud and clear at the universal exhibitions that punctuated the latter half of the 19th century. In Vienna in 1873, for instance, then in Paris in 1878—the same year in which the architect Domènech i Montaner published a crucial article in *La Renaixença* entitled *En busca de una arquitectura nacional* (In Search of a National Architecture)—and again in 1889, the Spanish pavilion on each occasion was built in the neo-Mudéjar style.

Like all major European cities, Barcelona has shops, pharmacies, cafés, and restaurants that bear witness to their proprietors' passing fancy for new forms. So it was when the Café Torino (below) was renovated in 1902. Many Catalan artists, including sculptor Eusebi Arnau and architect José Puig i Cadafalch, were called upon for their services. The mosaics and lamps were imported from Venice and the furniture was supplied by Thonet. Gaudí designed the motifs for the wall covering in the Arabic salon.

Gaudí's interpretation of the Mudéjar style

Several noticeably contemporary designs by Gaudí are habitually categorized as neo-Mudéjar, even though their "exotic" character is not in fact related to this trend alone. These are the summer residence built between 1883 and 1888 for the ceramic tile manufacturer Manuel Vicens Montaner; some pavilions at the second home of the Güell family, constructed between 1884 and 1887; and El Capricho, the summer villa at Comillas, 125 miles (200 km) from Barcelona, which was built between 1883 and 1885 for Don Máximo Díaz de Quijano.

What do these buildings have in common, and what do they owe to Moorish art? At first sight the towers, turrets and lanterns that characterize the outlines of each—in the case of El Capricho the tower can acccurately be described as a *mirador* (watchtower)—are unmistakeably reminiscent of the minarets and mosques of Cairo. Gaudí would have had no difficulty acquainting himself with these while still a student by consulting

The small coastal village of Comillas benefited from the enterprising spirit of one of its inhabitants, the merchant and financier Antonio López (1817–84). When he became the first Marquis of Comillas, López wished to endow his birthplace with buildings erected to his own glory, and turn it into an elite vacation resort. This strategy to gain recognition was highly successful; during the summer of 1881 the royal family stayed in the palace that López had had built there for his own use. (Above, the El Capricho villa.) Sculptors including Joan Llimona and Eusebi Arnau, and architects such as Martorell, Domènech i Montaner and Gaudí worked at Comillas.

books and photographs in the library at the Provincial School of Architecture.

On closer inspection, however, these various crowning structures are not precise reproductions of Moorish architectural features; they only suggest them in a general way, and are not attempts by the architect to reproduce them exactly. What Gaudí did, in an entirely eclectic manner, was to take elements almost at random—a cornice, a corbel, a molding, a finial—and combine them in his own particular way, with no real concern for stylistic coherence. Every element is given an existence in its own right, regardless of its formal isolation within the whole.

The same can be said of the often bold arrangement of materials and also therefore of the role played by polychromy. The facades of the Casa Vicens, for example, appear to be literally clothed in a garment cut out of a striped and checkered fabric. Bands of bricks and tiles of two types—some plain, others with floral patterns—are alternated in a highly skillful way that reveals Gaudí's outstanding talent as a colorist. The alternation is in no way systematic, however, and does not lead to any sense of monotony. Indeed, whereas on the first two levels of the house the axes are horizontal,

The obsession with color that the Casa Vicens (below left and above) displays has connections neither with historicism nor with eclecticism. It is much more closely related to the Western imagination, which throughout the 19th century had associated wealth, luxury, sumptuous materials, fantasy and fantastical forms with the East—a region that was usually known in the West through tales and travelers' accounts. Just like the Finca Güell, the Casa Vicens is an invitation to mental wandering and reverie; both offer a vision of the human dwelling freed from the contingencies of the present and the bourgeois world.

offered by industrial progress—the manufacture of metal in sheets and molded sections—as well as the traditional skills and expertise associated with working in wrought iron. The structure is made up of T- and L-shaped prefabricated pieces, and the monster's body is composed of an iron bar with a spring of varying thickness coiled around it. Its jointed claws are covered with scales made of repoussé sheet metal, and the foot on the left has a moving joint so that the claws rise up when the gate is opened.

The orange tree on top of the brick pillar next to the main gate and the lyre hanging from the small gate at the side have led some historians to see this gate as a work having symbolic resonance. These features may well be a reference to the priest-poet Jacint Verdaguer, who won the Floral Games in 1877 with an epic poem entitled *L'Atlantida*, recounting the labours of Hercules and the disappearance of Atlantis. In Canto X there appear a chained dragon and an orange tree recalling the famous Garden of the Hesperides of Greek mythology. Moreover, Verdaguer was a close friend of Eusebi Güell, for whom this virtuosic composition was created.

By using parabolic arches—which are neither fully semi-circular nor pointed—for the stables at the Finca Güell (above), Gaudí placed himself in the tradition of Catalan Gothic architecture. For example, the elongated novices' and monks' dormitories at the monastery in Poblet—which date from the 13th and 15th centuries—feature diaphragmlike arches that have an obvious parallel in Gaudí's design. Gaudí much admired this monastery, and had devised its lighting in 1882. Opposite page: a detail of the facade of the porter's lodge at the Finca Güell.

"I get this capacity to feel and see space from the fact that I am the son, grandson and great-grandson of a coppersmith. All these generations have prepared me. The coppersmith is a man who makes a three-dimensional object from a flat surface; he has seen the space before he starts his work. All the great Florentine artists of the Renaissance were carvers who created three-dimensional works from a plan."

It may have been this sense of heredity that led Gaudí to turn the practical business of ironwork into a spatial undertaking, in which he exploited fullness, emptiness, and depth. His staggering virtuosity in this medium can be seen in the stylized palm motifs on the outer railing at the Casa Vicens (page 35, below) and the dragons at the Finca Güell and the Casa Vicens (pages 34 and 35, above). According to Ricardo Opisso, Gaudí spent long hours in a forge in Carrer Roger de Flor. One day, becoming annoyed with a clumsy worker, he snatched the hammer from him and struck "apocalyptic blows on the anvil, starting with terrible fury and colossal power to straighten the incandescent iron and shape it as he wanted it."

An exceptional patron

Whatever its inspiration, this ensemble of pieces, although of modest proportions, proved that Gaudí had found in Güell a sponsor who was open to the most daring ideas. Eusebi Güell i Bacigalupi (1846–1918) was described by Gaudí as "a great lord, with the spirit of a prince, like that of the Medici of Florence and the Dorias of Genoa". He was certainly an ideal patron, who allowed the architect's genius to express itself in complete freedom. During the 1870s Güell took part in the political life of Barcelona, but it was mainly to his business activities that he owed his power and influence.

Eusebi Güell was in charge of major textile concerns whose productivity was spectacularly increased by new machines and production techniques that were introduced by one of his colleagues, Ferran Alsina, who was renowned for his scientific approach to industry.

It was for the "Doge," as Gaudí liked to call Güell, that from 1886 to 1889 the architect built an urban palace—the Palau Güell—that, with regard to its

structure and its component parts, as well as the handling of space, was highly innovatory. For the first time, Gaudí was also confronted by the issue of interior decoration, in this case on a quite exceptional scale, and set about solving it in a sumptuous fashion. The interior of the palace was in striking contrast to the severity of the exterior, which at first sight brings to mind the Venetian Gothic style but which in fact owes more to the influence of Viollet-le-Duc. The Palau Güell was used as a residence but also for receptions. It comprises six levels, including a remarkable basement that contained the stables and was reached by a spiral ramp supported by cylindrical brick pillars crowned by capitals in the shape of flattened cones. Upstairs, the hall at the very center of the building is crowned by a huge double-shell dome pierced by many small, circular holes. The hall contains a chapel and leads in to the drawing room, which is in turn connected to a private drawing room and a billiards room.

This level is reached by the main staircase which, starting on the first floor, leads up to a lobby opening on to a drawing room and a reception room. The upper floors are filled with bedrooms designed for the masters of the house and their guests and servants.

The facade is entirely devoid of sculpture or polychrome elements, apart from a single decorative feature at the entrance—a colossal wrought-iron emblem of Catalonia. Its severity is increased by the covering of undressed stone that here and there interrupts the marble of the first floor, the mezzanine and the columns of the huge gallery running almost the whole length of the second and third floors.

Most of the furniture designed for the Palau Güell is in the neo-Gothic and neo-Rococo style. This is not surprising considering that Eusebi Güell wanted the palace to be a place where he could house and display his

In 1888, although the interior of his palace was not completely finished, Eusebi Güell gave a reception there in honor of the royal family. The Palau Güell was a building designed primarily for social gatherings (right: the hall). The decision to locate it on La Rambla, the main thoroughfare of the historic city center, was due to Güell's desire for his palace to follow in the tradition of the prestigious residences of the 18th century. Güell was often caricatured in the Barcelona press. Here he is shown walking past the pavilion at the entrance to his park, carrying baskets of *rovellones* (Catalan mushrooms)—an allusion to certain architectural features of the park.

collections of early art, in which medieval Catalan art took pride of place. Some of the furniture, however, marked a complete departure from everything that had so far been produced in the genre of furnishings. One chaise longue, for instance, exhibits a complete contrast between its very comfortable upholstery and its wrought-iron frame, which is conceived along entirely different lines. Likewise, there is a washstand that looks as if it might topple over at any moment; the intentionally lopsided mirror makes any symmetry impossible, while the base suggests the movement of a

running animal. These are completely original designs whose highly fanciful quality finds an echo in the "Oriental" splendor of the little gables, each one different from the rest, that crown the numerous chimneys and ventilation ducts that are dotted about the flat roof like pieces on a bizarre chessboard. They anticipate the even more astonishing assemblage of shapes that, a few years later, would rise up from the undulating roof of the Casa Milá—which would take on the appearance of a labyrinth from ancient times populated with impassive, mysterious, helmeted warriors.

"Could anyone create anything more original than this collection of fantastical chimneys made from leftover scraps of building material? The fragments of glass, unwanted pieces of marble, broken *azulejos* (glazed ceramic tiles) and bits of limekiln are randomly pieced together into ingenious, fanciful forms that make up a brilliant ensemble with a wealth of color, and demonstrate that a true artist can make beauty spring even from debris."

La Vanguardia
3 August 1890
(The writer was Frederic Rahola, the secretary of a protectionist employers' organization and connected to Eusebi Güell through politics and business.)

Despite the sumptuous "baroque" character of the interior decoration of the Palau Güell, the Palladian influence on the scheme for the great central hall, and the striking originality of some of the building's spaces, how much this architecture owes to the neo-Gothic style is beyond doubt. Gaudí undertook nothing less than a revision of the Gothic, ultimately concluding that it was certainly a style, albeit not an entirely successful one: "Gothic art is imperfect…it is geometric, formulaic, with endless repetition."

CHAPTER 3

GOTHIC AND RATIONALISM

Although poverty was one of the rules of the Order of St Teresa of Avila, and the material used in the construction of the Colegio Teresiano was of an unusually thrifty nature, Gaudí gave the building a certain majesty, which can be seen very clearly in the crenellations on the roof (left). Right: the capital of a column in the hallway of the Palacio Episcopal in Astorga, León.

Gaudí never attempted to conceal the debt that he owed to Eugène Viollet-le-Duc, and to his theoretical writings in particular. Although the restorations carried out by Viollet-le-Duc between 1860 and 1877 on the Cathedral of Saint-Sernin in Toulouse were a disappointment to Gaudí, he found the *Dictionnaire raisonné de l'architecture française* extremely helpful, especially at the time when he was designing the Palau Güell.

DICTIONNAIRE RAISONNÉ
DE
L'ARCHITECTURE
FRANÇAISE
DU XIe AU XVIe SIÈCLE
PAR
E. VIOLLET-LE-DUC

TOME DEUXIÈME

PARIS
ERNEST GRÜND

To help them formulate their conception of "modernity," late 19th-century architects could turn to the theoretical writings of Eugène Viollet-le-Duc (below). His ten-volume *Dictionnaire raisonné de l'architecture française* (left), published from 1854 to 1868, provided a remarkably useful approach and point of reference, whose virtues they in turn extolled.

The single element that lends variety to the building's austere, elongated facade—the narrow, closed, projecting gallery lined with a series of columns—could easily have been inspired by the elevation of a medieval house in Cluny drawn by Viollet-le-Duc.

It is also quite possible that the plan for the great central hall, although ostensibly suggestive of Palladio, can be traced back to Viollet-le-Duc; in the 19th of his *Entretiens sur l'architecture* (Discussions on Architecture), published in 1863, he praised the rationality of the internal layout of an English building, Warkworth Castle; this was organized around a central well which incorporated the staircase and was covered by a lantern.

A child of Viollet-le-Duc

The shadow of Viollet-le-Duc hovers over two other buildings by Gaudí, which he began to plan after the Palau Güell had entered the construction stage: these were the Palacio Episcopal (Bishop's

Palace) in Astorga, León, built between 1887 and 1893, and the Colegio Teresiano (College of the Teresians, the sisters of St Teresa of Avila), which was built in Barcelona in record time from 1888 to 1890. The idea of a rectangular structure of extreme simplicity, which characterizes both buildings, may have come from sketches and commentaries given in the *Dictionnaire* in relation to the kitchens and infirmary of the Abbey of Sainte-Marie de Breteuil in the *département* of Oise, in Normandy.

Here Gaudí also used the central lightwell, a device that he had used at the Palau Güell. It was perhaps with the building of the Colegio Teresiano, commissioned by

On all four facades of the Colegio Teresiano and on every floor, the windows take the form of pointed arches. In strong counteraction to this motif are the rectangular outlines of the wooden shutters, which are often closed, and the assertive hexagon of the projecting gallery at the entrance.

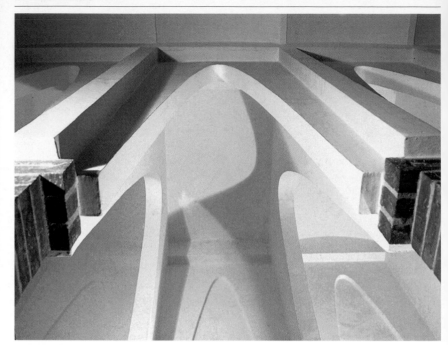

Don Enrique de Ossó, the founder of the order, that Gaudí came closest to Viollet-le-Duc in the extent to which the ultimate result met the various demands of a building whose dominant themes were meditation, reflection, and austerity. These characteristics are clearly apparent when one looks at this gigantic, hexagonal structure that is pierced by a sequence of identical windows repeated in an imperturbable, regular rhythm on all four of the facades.

The Order of St Teresa did not of course have the same financial means as an industrial magnate. As a result Gaudí chose as his material a rough, rubble stone masonry for the first three floors, while the fourth was built entirely of industrial bricks. He also used bricks to frame every aperture and to create a decorative band, adorned with the order's emblem in blood-red ceramics, between each story. Since this was an establishment intended for the education of both resident and

On the upper level of the Colegio Teresiano, the brickwork of the tall parabolic arches that line the corridors, unlike those on the ground floor, are covered in a fine coating of white plaster, forming the sort of large white surfaces that are frequently found in Mujédar art. As a result the light, which at this point streams in at an oblique angle, is greatly increased.

nonresident novices, the architect considered the most effective ways of facilitating movement around the building, as well as accommodation and lighting. The classrooms are located on the two middle floors, while the bedrooms are on the two topmost floors.

In order to allow light to flood into the work areas, the windows are larger on the lower floors. On the lowest floor, a central corridor runs from one end of the building to the other and gives access to the classrooms, while on the ground floor two similar corridors run on either side of an inner courtyard, which also serves as a source of light. Although this is a minimal, highly rationalist space which could easily have been designed for an industrial building, it is strongly marked by Gaudí's genius in the handling of solid forms. Once again the desire, already seen at the Finca Güell, to round the angles of the external walls is apparent. Here the empty space on the two topmost floors extends into the towers at the end, and the cavity thus created is used to display the order's emblem, which seems to float in the air like a banner. The most striking stamp of Gaudí's personality, however, is the substitution of the Gothic arch for the signature parabolic arch; on the building's exterior, these arches give the windows their very particular exterior shape, while in the interior, raised so as to minimize lateral stress, they create long, cloister-like corridors that are more conducive to novices' reflection and meditation than to playful frolics.

As at the Palau Güell, the austerity of the main façade of the Colegio Teresiano is tempered by an imposing double portal in wrought iron, which fills the lower part of the parabolic arch at the entrance. There are also wrought-iron bars on the parabolic windows on the ground floor; the design of the windows incorporates the initials of Jesus Christ.

A challenging project

The fact that no such arches are to be seen in the Palacio Episcopal in Astorga is surprising. There, as in the Colegio Teresiano and the Palau Güell, the building's internal space is organized around a large central cavity. A lightwell whose sides are formed by a staircase effectively constitutes the center of the building, while the topmost floor is a single, large empty space; the walls of this upper story consist of windows, which allow so much light to flood in that the space seems ethereal. Because Monsignor Joan Baptista Grau, the bishop who had commissioned the palace, died in 1893, before it was completed, Gaudí did not remain in complete control of the project. At that point the cathedral chapter, urged on by local builders who were jealous of the privileges enjoyed by the workmen whom Gaudí had brought from Barcelona, gave notice to the architect and his team. Nevertheless, the palace, with its highly uniform facades, markedly vertical lines and elegant turrets, remains a very fine example of an entirely orthodox neo-Gothic building.

This setback did not in any way prevent Gaudí from continuing his work in León. He then turned to building the Casa de Los Botines, in the city's historic center, for two friends of Eusebi Güell, the textile merchants Fernández and Andrés. As in several private houses in Barcelona, Gaudí used the ground floor for offices in which the owners could conduct their

Because of heavy snowfalls in León, Gaudí gave the Casa de Los Botines (above) a fine covering of slate and set the corner towers with steeply pitched roofs. The formula became very popular and was adopted by other architects in Barcelona. This made Gaudí say with a wry smile: "They are being over-cautious; they are putting pointed towers on their buildings in case the climate changes."

business, while the upper stories were given over to numerous connecting apartments. From a formal point of view, the imposing, compact mass of this building also makes it classifiable as being in the neo-Gothic style. Here the vertical dynamic so beloved of the architect is less apparent than usual and is expressed only in certain elements of the building—the dormer windows, the chimneys, and especially the corner turrets—which are clearly of French inspiration and are once again arranged in such a way as to make any angular junction between the walls impossible. The building gives an unusual sense of powerful

Unusually for him, Gaudí used white granite for the Palacio Episcopal in Astorga. A deep ditch was dug around the building, and as a result the various towers seem to spring abruptly out of the earth. The sculptures at the entrance were initially intended as finials for the towers.

horizontality, which is reinforced by the uninterrupted sequence of dripstones on the lower stories.

A secular Gothic architecture

Thus, however much Gaudí had learned from Viollet-le-Duc's ideas, through his own interpretation he was modifying them to a remarkable degree. For all that he had pondered it, Gaudí's approach to the Gothic style cannot be reduced to theoretical knowledge taken from books; it came about naturally in the course of his work. As a student he took part in field trips organized by Elies Rogent at the Provincial School of Architecture, and therefore had the opportunity very early on to become familiar with the Gothic style not only in Catalonia but also in Roussillon. Later he stayed in the city of León and was able to take time to study its cathedral, which is a jewel of Gothic architecture and a fine example of the influence of the French School. He also went to Burgos but, much to the disappointment of its leading citizens, he found the cathedral's richness deliberately ostentatious.

Much later, Gaudí paid homage to the Catalan Gothic style with the Torre Bellesguard, the country house that he built from 1900 to 1905 in Carrer Bellesguard on the outskirts of Barcelona. It was commissioned by María Sagués, a member of a family that favored the restoration of the Church of

The ground plan of the cathedral of Santa María de Régia in León (above) is thought to be based on Reims Cathedral, whereas its elevation is reminiscent of Amiens. Work on the cathedral began in 1205 and continued until the beginning of the 14th century. After being altered in later periods, it was restored to its original condition in the 19th century.

Catalonia's role in politics, and was located on the very site where, according to tradition, Marti I, the last king of the Catalan dynasty, had built a residence in 1408. As a symbol of a Catalan past that had to be defended, the house itself took on a defensive character. This is expressed by the harshness and austerity of its lines (the angles are accentuated in a way that is thoroughly unusual for Gaudí), by its crenellations and machicolations, and by its very narrow windows, suggesting the loophole windows in the walls of a fortress, and also by the sturdy slanting pillars that line the path leading up to the residence. The interior, however, is marked by features highly typical of Gaudí's style, such as the intertwined ribbed vaulting on the *piano nobile* (the main, upper floor) and the spiral columns in the attic gallery.

With its square, highly compact design and tower crowned by a ceramic cross whose arms face toward the four points of the compass, Torre Bellesguard (above) stands like a monolith in the Catalan landscape. Although Gaudí built it from humble local schist, he succeeded in creating a delicate range of colors in shades of gray, green, brown, and yellow.

The inspiration of the Baroque spirit

At the time that he was building the Torre Bellesguard, Gaudí had already explored new avenues that drew him away from the neo-Gothic and led to the construction of the Casa Calvet, named for Pedro Calvet, the textile manufacturer who commissioned it. This commission, which occupied him from 1898 to 1904, gave Gaudí the opportunity to work on a type of project that he had not yet tackled: namely a townhouse that was to form part of an alignment of buildings along a street. The facade of the Casa Calvet is of undressed stone, and the key elements of the scheme are a bay window above the entrance, and a pair of crowning gables. The relentless regularity of the windows is alleviated by the trilobate balconies, which draw attention to the two vertical rows of windows on either side of the gallery. What distinguishes this facade from anything that Gaudí had previously designed is its sculpted ornamentation. The gables have

The austere, angular forms of the exterior of the Torre Bellesguard are in striking contrast to the shapes and decoration of the interior. This is particularly noticeable in the lobby, where the corbeled pillars and ceilings prefigure the undulating forms of the Casa Milá. Covered in smooth white roughcast, walls and ceilings merge into one another, the angles between them being rounded, so that the play of light and shadow softens the concrete elements.

cruciform finials and above each of the windows on the topmost story are busts of the patron saint of the owner and of his native village, surmounted by the palms of martyrdom. The gallery is decorated with a mesmerizing profusion of plant motifs that can be traced to *moergulas*, mushrooms known as "devil's eggs," that also appear in the wrought-iron nodes of the balustrades. Wrought iron is also the material of the plate bearing the number of the house, the bell push-buttons, the front door handle, and, most strikingly, of the strange cruciform door knockers that, when they are taken in the hand, come crashing down on a monstrous louse.

The interior holds further surprises, most notably in the lobby, which leads to the stairwell and elevator. With a wrought-iron grille surrounded by balusters topped by Ionic capitals and flanked by corkscrew columns marking the entrance to the stairwell, this room is nothing less than a Baroque baldachin.

This small area is preceded by a vestibule in which space is broken up by the use of mirrors. The latter reflect not only each other but also the three lamps decorated with volutes and crowns that are fixed to their frames. The Casa Calvet also enabled Gaudí to

The facade of the Casa Calvet (below), sandwiched between two existing buildings, was awarded a prize by Barcelona's city council. It was the only official mark of recognition that Gaudí received in his lifetime.

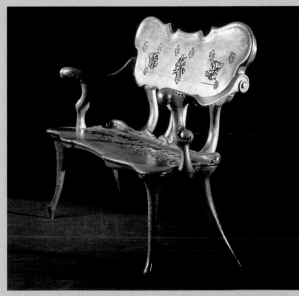

Given its whimsical forms suggesting mineral rocks, fossils, and the human skeleton, it is easy to lose sight of the fact that the office furniture made for the Casa Calvet was also the product of ergonomic research. The skillfully designed curves ensure the most comfortable sitting position possible, giving excellent support to the lumbar vertebrae in particular. The furniture was designed and made with remarkable precision and in a rigorously rationalistic manner. In order to give them maximum strength, infinite care was taken over the shaping and assembly of the various components of the seats and backs of the chairs, as well as the joints and points at which the various sections of the frame are attached. Joan Bergós, who was once a disciple of Gaudí, recounted a very revealing anecdote in relation to this. During the Spanish Civil War, the windows on the upper floor of the Casa Calvet were blown in, and an office chair that happened to have been placed behind one of the panes was hit by the blast. Instead of being smashed to pieces, the chair simply came apart at the joints and could be put back together without the slightest difficulty.

Several pieces of furniture that Gaudí designed for the Palau Güell, including an armchair for the drawing room (far left) and the dressing table for Señora Güell's bedroom (below left), fall within the 18th-century *rocaille* tradition that in the eyes of the pan-European middle-class clientele of the time was firmly established as the preeminent aristocratic style. The Calvet family also owned "neo-Rococo" furniture designed by Gaudí, including a mirror in carved and gilt wood (detail, above left), which was probably made in the workshops of Joan Busquets. Despite their highly fanciful nature, these pieces have undeniably ergonomic qualities. That is certainly true of the two enormous armchairs covered in Córdoba leather; although the curves and countercurves of their carved and gilt ornaments are clearly in the Rococo spirit, those that shape the back and the seat are designed to fit the body of the occupant perfectly and even to lend a certain elegance to the sitter's position. The small shelf on the base of the dressing table was specially designed to make it easier for the lady to lace her boots.

develop his designs for furniture. The seating furniture that he produced for the drawing room of the apartment conceived for the use of Calvet and his family was similar to that at the Palau Güell. As before, great importance was attached to the upholstery of the seat and back of the chairs, and to the material of the frame (of carved and gilt wood), both of which produced a very rich impression; the feet, however, which are decorated with floral motifs fashioned in metal, are in the form of spirals; any suspicion that these pieces might be overstated is banished by this very daring device.

The real innovation here, which led Gaudí in directions that he would ceaselessly explore from then on, was the furniture that he designed for the office and the shop on the first floor of the Casa Calvet—and his use of direct manual action in order to determine form. The story goes that, to design the handles for the doors on the landing, Gaudí stuck his hands into some soft clay and used the impression that they left as the basis for the design. As to the office furniture at the Casa Calvet—the pieces have strongly functional frames and bonelike joints, which bring to mind the human skeleton—it was full of a powerful sense of vitality that was soon to pervade Gaudí's entire architectural style.

For the design of the lobby at the Casa Calvet (left), Gaudí turned to the great Spanish Baroque tradition. The elevator is ceremonially presented in the manner of an altar, and shows similarities to 18th-century Catalan altarpieces, particularly those of the sculptor Lluís Bonifàs (1730–86). Above: the central bay window above the main entrance.

During the early years of the 20th century, Gaudí succeeded in fusing the temperament of a born builder with his bold vision in the handling of three-dimensional forms. Freed from the opposition between the structure of a building and its decoration, his architectural style achieved an entirely fresh formal unity. The stone of which his buildings consist becomes an organic, living mass infused with a pulsing dynamism that is unique in the history of architecture.

CHAPTER 4
TOWARD AN ORGANIC ARCHITECTURE

"Architecture must not renounce color, but must on the contrary use it to bring shape and physical volume to life. Color is the complement of form, and the clearest manifestation of life."
Gaudí

Right: a medallion on the ceiling of the market at Park Güell. Left, a detail of the roof of Casa Batlló.

The year 1900 marked the beginning of the largest project Gaudí ever directed in Barcelona: Park Güell. The whole area, covering about 50 acres (20 hectares) on the south side of the Muntanya Pelada, which rises on the northwest side of the city, was listed as a World Heritage Site by UNESCO in 1984. Although it has become a park in the true sense of the word and is very popular with the people of Barcelona as somewhere pleasant to walk, it was not originally designed as such. It was in fact intended as a real garden city, inspired by English models; this explains the spelling of the word "park," which was used by Gaudí himself on the plan that he submitted for the approval of the mayor of Barcelona. Thus what Eusebi Güell, the owner of the land, and Gaudí, assisted by José Pardo Casanovas and Julian Bardié Pardo, had planned to create on the rocky mountain-

side was a residential area, set well away from the city and overlooked by a chapel. The project failed, however, owing to the rather mixed reception that it received; of the 60 plots intended for private dwellings, only two were sold and built on.

Nature set in stone

Park Güell nevertheless remains a dazzling demonstration of Gaudí's genius. This is apparent first in the way in which he addressed the problems posed by terrain that was rather difficult to move around in and whose layout made it awkward to create the embankments and platforms without which any architectural construction was impossible.

To avoid installing costly stone terraces, Gaudí had the idea of building three viaducts on different levels. The lowest one consists of two rows of inward-slanting columns whose shafts widen at the top so as to join seamlessly with the arch, thus creating a parabolic shape.

In 1903 the Association of Catalan Architects visited the construction site of Park Güell. Salvador Sellés was their spokesman: "The load-bearing, slanting columns come in various sections; some are worked with refinement, all are agreeably rustic, some are spiral and some cylindrical. Some are reinforced on the outside so that they look like stalactites and stalagmites that have been carved by a whim of nature."

These columns have no base, and rise out of the ground
like tree trunks. The other viaducts each have three rows
of columns: one central, vertical row and two lateral,
inward-sloping rows. Whereas in the lower viaduct the
stones on the columns are arranged in such a way as to
suggest stalactites, here they support ribbed vaulting.

The columns also have bases and capitals that clearly
refer to the typology of an architectural order. Each of
these covered walkways also has a different finish.
The shafts on the lower level are covered with uneven
stones arranged so as to suggest the bark and branches
of a palm tree. On the upper levels the stones are flat
and regular, although the effect is rustic. There is
another allusion to nature in the rows of monumental
flower tubs made of coarse, undressed stone that
border the highest viaduct. These look very much like
a row of trees: trees made of stone, of course, but
brought to life by the agaves that were planted at the
top of them.

There is a real dialogue here between natural and
architectural forms. This is reinforced by the choice of

"Here a strange animal, there a head, further on a mummified caryatid, produced by a new technique of compressing a number of pieces together by the force of cement...Many of them will feel the roots of palm trees brushing against them as these roots search out crevices so as to absorb the liquids and substances that they need for their foliage to grow. All of them will give to those they shelter a natural decoration that looks like the dreams of an ardent imagination."

Salvador Sellés

Below: Count Güell in 1915, leaning against one of the columns in the great central hall.

plants—pines, carobs, palms, grasses and scrub—and of construction materials, whose color and irregular texture blend into the landscape like the great dry-stone constructions of the Tarragona region that probably figured in Gaudí's mind.

By contrast, an apparently much more orthodox architectural style can be found in the great columned hall that was originally intended to house the market where the future residents of Park Güell would come to do their shopping. The columns—of which there are more than 90—clearly refer to the Doric model as described by the Roman architect and engineer Vitruvius.

Gaudí nevertheless introduced several modifications; the diameter of

"The most synthetic architectonic constructions that have been made until this day are to be found at Park Güell, a glorious page, if ever there was one, in the broad history of architecture. These are the first manifestations of a whole architectural cycle that everyone wants to see grow, and perhaps the most transcendental of the fruits that our renaissance has produced. These plastic

the columns is significantly larger than that of their classical prototypes, while their fluting (vertical grooving) is wider, the molding of the cornices thicker and the neck-moldings flattened, giving an impression of massiveness that is far removed from the refinement of the Greek model. Moreover, the guttae hanging from the triglyphs of the frieze and the cornice are less stylized and more naturalistic. In reality, Gaudí created a new architectural order here, suggesting the remote times when architecture was born.

The columned hall gives an impression of mysterious solemnity. This is in stark contrast to the luminous gaiety of the esplanade that the columns support. This extensive area has a beaten earth surface and is encircled by a bench—completely covered with broken ceramic tiles and pieces of glass—that snakes along its winding perimeter like a gigantic reptile.

This *trencadís* is also the material that forms the skin of a giant salamander in the fountain set at the center of the steps leading to the hall. Its symbolic role is comparable to that of Python, the serpent of Greek mythology that was the guardian of the precious subterranean waters; the water flowing from the salamander's mouth comes from a 2640-gallon (12,000-liter) cistern. There are more *trencadís* at the top of the outer wall, which has seven gates and undulates with the contours of the land, as well as on the walls flanking the stairway at the main entrance and on the roofs of the two pavilions there. The latter have an oval ground plan and are enclosed within the wall itself. One of them was the porter's lodge; the other, topped by a tower 33 feet (10 meters) tall and completely covered in *trencadís*, was intended to house the administrative services of the garden city.

Architecture and decoration become one

Those fragments of colored tile were not used in any haphazard way. Their arrangement was the result of

forms, these stone creations, are the visible and palpable sign of the renewal of our practical, idealistic and scientific spirit, which loves flying off to distant horizons and finding practical, simple means of producing grandiose effects."
        Joan Rubió,
    architect and one of
        Gaudí's assistants,
*Problems in Achieving
Architectonic Synthesis*
        (1913)

both a profound reflection on the role of color in architecture and of a sensitive empiricism. This is borne out by a statement made by a mason who worked on the Casa Batlló, particularly in covering the facade with a revetment of *trencadís* consisting of a combination of ceramic disks and pieces of glass: "Don Antón stood in the middle of the road in front of the house and shouted out from there where we should put the various pieces. But, for masons who were used to working on regular mosaics, it wasn't easy to adapt to a new technique, especially working with so many colors. We often had to take down whole sections until he was satisfied." Joan Bergós also recalled that on the outer edge of the disks "were painted the basic shades selected by the architect himself. According to the indications given by these brushmarks, the workmen put in place shards of glass of the same shade, decreasing in intensity until they were toned down to the light grays of the background."

Gaudí was commissioned to build this house in 1904 by the wealthy industrialist José Batlló i Casanovas. It was not in fact so much a question of building a new house as of altering an existing one dating from the 1870s. The architect's task

"It was therefore a question of constructing a building that was habitable (and also, in my opinion, edible) and that suggested the reflections of twilight clouds on the waters of a lake. It was simultaneously to have the utmost naturalism and the greatest trompe-l'oeil effects. I proclaim that this gigantic project was simply based on Rimbaud's submersion of a drawing room at the bottom of a lake." Thus Salvador Dalí defined the design of the Casa Batlló. Above left: a detail of the rooftop.

was to extend and modernize the entire building. This involved adding two extra stories, reworking the revetment of the facade, and converting the third floor into an apartment for the owner to live in. That a simple conversion should have led to so much innovation is quite astonishing. The building's novelty lies largely in the joyful polychromy of the facade, which cuts into the facades of the neighboring houses—including the famous Casa Amatler, built several years before by Josep Puig i Cadafalch—and which glitters in the sun, as do the enameled roof tiles that suggest the iridescent scales and backbone of a fairytale saurian.

It is said that, much to Gaudí's delight, an English architect passing through Barcelona exclaimed: "This house looks like something out of Hansel and Gretel!"

Equally novel was the undulating rhythm, similar to that of the line of the rooftop, that runs through the jambs, balconies, and transoms of Montjuich stone. From these, other elements protrude. The columns on the ground floor jut out almost 2 feet (60 centimeters) on to the sidewalk; this led to objections from the

On several occasions Gaudí criticized classical architecture, in which he said that "the false distinction between the supporting and load-bearing elements creates an imperfect discontinuity between the upright or column and the arch or lintel. Attempts are then made to conceal this discontinuity with such decorative additions as capitals, consoles and transoms." At the Casa Batlló, however, the various elements that make up the facade fit together, link with one another and, despite their powerful originality, fuse to the extent of losing their individuality to create a rhythmic unity.

highways department, which Gaudí ignored. These features do not have the appearance of being attached to the facade but seem to rise up from inside the house and to tear through its colored skin. The shape of these stone elements is also powerfully original and richly suggestive; they may have come from the inert world of mineral rocks, but their fluidity and suppleness, almost their softness, suggests the vital, palpitating organs on which human life depends.

José Battló's personal apartment echoes the rhythm of the facade. Here, the undulating lines have entered the house— or perhaps they come out from within it—and progress according to the laws of the cellular world. The rooms follow on from one another in the way that organic cells grow.

The dragon's backbone on the roof reappears in the banisters of the staircase leading up to the apartment. This is a universe from which right angles and flat surfaces are relentlessly banned. The ceilings and walls are molded, while the panels and interconnecting doors are rounded. In the interests of ergonomics, deriving from research carried out in connection with the office furniture at the Casa Calvet, the furniture in the drawing room and dining room has developed slightly slanting planes and imperceptibly convex and concave surfaces. The chairs invite one to sit on them, or even

In José Battló's apartment, it seems as if the plaster on the ceilings has escaped from the upper levels and liquefied, leaving folds, wrinkles, and whirlpools along the way, and is in the process of continuing its descent down the wood paneling and the doors. The ceilings at the Casa Milá are even more tormented, here and there revealing real yawning gaps with multiple configurations.

give the impression that they have taken on the shape of the bodies of people who have sat on them. The wood appears to be arrested in a state of liquefaction, as does the stone of the arches and pillars on the facade. Strictly resisting straight lines, the wood paneling, door jambs and window frames are in keeping with the undulating walls, echoing them in the interior space of the house, which in places is run through by a centrifugal force; the ceiling of the drawing room looks

Photographs taken at the time (page 70 and page 72, above) give a very precise idea of the atmosphere created in the furnished spaces designed by Gaudí for José Batlló. Nothing similar exists for Casa Calvet, and there is very little documentation

as if it had been sucked in by a typhoon and stirred up by a violent whirlwind. Gaudí doubtless had in mind a remark made to him by his assistant, the sculptor Josep Llimona (1864–1943): "Things dipped in soft paste give the impression that they are hanging in the air or in a nebula."

regarding the interior of the Palau Güell. For the Casa Milá, all that remains are documents relating to its construction. Extant views of the interior date from a later time when Señora Milá had the furniture designed by Gaudí, including the screen (page 73, below), replaced by period furniture and seating upholstered with fabrics of classic design (page 72, below).

A fluid architecture in homage to the Virgin

Gaudí developed these undulating rhythms on an infinitely grander scale when, some years later, he undertook the construction of an apartment block for the ceramics manufacturers Pere Milá i Camps and Roser Segimón, creating a building that is without

The door jambs and seats that Gaudí designed for the Casa Batlló are truly tactile entities. They elicit an irresistible desire to run one's fingers along armrests and around the edges of seats, backs, and frames so as to feel the slightest inflections in the line, and detect the imperceptibly convex and concave relief of apparently flat surfaces. In this respect these pieces have something in common with the endless bench at Park Güell. Certain details of the furniture at the Casa Batlló also suggest the mineral world—for instance, in the fossil-like ornamentation on the upper edge of the backs of the dining room chairs. The long seven-seater bench beneath the huge mirror whose divisions echo those of the window opposite and of the door to its right, and the window in the corner of the room that continues the same rhythm, have affinities with a geological world shaped by the effects of erosion and gullying in a way that is ergonomically pleasing. Page 72: an interior at the Casa Batlló (above) and the Casa Milá (below).

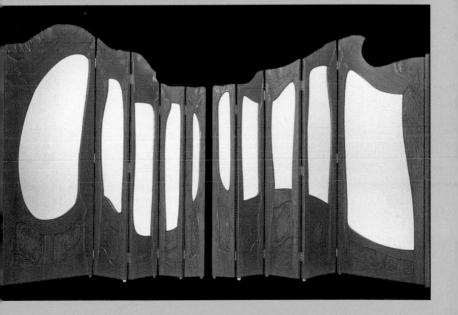

equivalent anywhere in the world.

The very real concerns that Gaudí had regarding its construction found remarkably ingenious solutions, such as the enlargement of the lightwell in the upper stories. But any such problems were completely swallowed up in a physical mass that suggests a gigantic sculpture worked in soft clay rather than a house. Gaudí began by radically altering the site on which the house was to stand. He obliterated the angle that was formed by two intersecting streets and raised a rounded building with a single, continuous facade that forms an extensive bare surface through which runs a continuous visual rhythm.

In place of polychromy, Gaudí used just one material—a stone that was originally creamy white,

Republican newspapers often published caricatures of Gaudí. Here (left) he is shown hoisting a statue of the Virgin to the top of the Casa Milá, under the benevolent eye of the Bishop of Barcelona. The Casa Milá, shown below in a drawing by Joan Matamala, was also the object of jibes, being described as a "Trojan horse without riders," a "cavernous ocean," and a "zeppelin garage." "It's a dinosaur cave," exclaimed Georges Clémenceau, the future prime minister of France, when he passed through Barcelona in late 1910.

hence the building's nickname, La Pedrera (The Quarry). The illusion is of an architectural entity bodily removed from an arid landscape such as the rocky area of San Miguel de Fay located about 12 miles (20 kilometers) north of Barcelona and well known to Gaudí. He himself suggested this on several occasions; for example in a conversation he had with the painter Carlès on the roof of the Casa Milà: "How," the young man asked him, "do you justify the curvilinear forms and volumes of this façade?" "They are justified because they are connected to those of the Collcerola and Tibidabo mountains that you can see from here."

Gaudí's contemporaries, impressed by the telluric force emanating from the building, made endless comparisons between it and the animal, vegetable, and mineral kingdoms, as if the architect were a descendant of the Titans or of Richard Wagner.

It should not be forgotten that the house was originally conceived as an homage to the Virgin Mary, whose image was to crown the façade. The sculptor Carlos Maní (1866–1911) had produced a model of

"I designed this work as a monument to the Virgin of the Rosary, because Barcelona did not have enough monuments." According to architect Joan Bassegoda, the wrought-iron elements that decorate the balconies were created by the Badia brothers from a proto type (the central balcony three levels above the entrance) and were made under Gaudí's super-vision and according to his instructions. This invalidates the opinion of several architectural historians who see these pieces as the contri-bution of architect Josep María Jujol, who worked with Gaudí on the building .

the group, with the Virgin carrying the Infant Jesus in her arms, which was to have been created in stone, gilt metal, and glass. This fact allows a slightly different interpretation of the building: the undulations of the facade, which decrease in size as the stories rise, may represent the swell of the Mediterranean Sea, the waves approaching, lapping and coming to die at the feet of the Virgin. Because of the anticlerical riots that took place in July 1909 and that led to about 50 religious establishments being burned down, the businessmen for whom the Casa Milá had been built abandoned the

idea of the sculpture, and of the little tower dedicated to the Virgin that had been intended to flank the facade.

Disappointed by this reaction, Gaudí lost interest in the project, handing its direction over to one of his assistants, the young architect Josep María Jujol (1879–1949). From then on, his spiritual force and Christian lyricism were devoted to the impossible completion of an enterprise on which he had already been working for over 20 years: the great Templo Expiatorio de la Sagrada Familia.

The roof terrace at the Casa Milá (above left and above) is certainly one of the most dream-like spaces that Gaudí created, but its dreaminess is not without a strong sense of insecurity. This is because the roof terrace takes the form of an outer path, with an uneven surface, that encircles two inner courtyards without the safety of a railing. Dotted about are chimneys and ventilation ducts that have become mysterious, perhaps even disquieting, helmeted silhouettes. Below left: a historical view of the entrance to the circular patio on the first level.

By devoting himself singlemindedly to the construction of the Sagrada Familia, Gaudí aimed to breathe new life into the Gothic style, which he admired but which he regarded as being formulaic: "Overthrowing three centuries of architecture is a titanic task for one man, but that does not mean that we should not undertake it."

CHAPTER 5
THE HELLENIC TEMPLE OF MEDITERRANEAN GOTHIC

The building of the church of the Sagrada Familia is a project that has continuously developed as it progressed, even during Gaudí's lifetime. Gaudí abandoned his original idea that the Nativity Facade should have a large number of towers with Gothic pinnacles, as in the recent model that can be seen today in the crypt (right). Left, the Nativity Facade as it appeared in the 1960s.

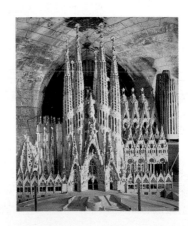

It was as the result of a private initiative that, in the fall of 1883, Gaudí agreed to lead this construction project, having been approached by Joan Martorell, the advisor on the project. The initiative came from the bookseller and publisher Josep María Bocabella, who after the cholera epidemic of the summer of 1865 had founded the Asociación Espiritual de Devotos de San José to raise funds to build a church dedicated to St Joseph and the Holy Family. By 1881 the funds had been raised,

In 1905 the poet Joan Maragall recalled the genesis of the Sagrada Familia: "From the dark back room of a shop in the old town, a very humble man came out with a great idea to build a new cathedral, and with a tiny sum of money raised through charity, the glorious work began, beneath the ground in a distant suburb that at the time was still in the middle of the country." The man in question was Josep María Bocabella (above, in a portrait by Aleix Clapés). As early as 1869 he had published a work advocating the building of the expiatory temple. The construction site of the Sagrada Familia was the object of numerous official visits. Members of the royal family, aristocrats, religious and political dignitaries, and students too, had the emerging building explained to them by Gaudí. Left: Gaudí in conversation with Cardinal Ragonesi, papal nuncio, and the Bishop of Barcelona.

and once a site on the edge of the Eixample had been purchased, approaches were made to the diocesan architect Francesc de Paula del Villar, who produced a plan for a church in the neo-Gothic style. The first stone was laid in 1882, on St Joseph's Day. A few months later, when the crypt had already been excavated and the pillars erected, Villar had a disagreement with Martorell and resigned from his post.

A spiritual commitment

Gaudí immediately set to work with an enthusiasm that was all the greater because this was for him an opportunity to use art, his art, in the service of religion. Another question arises: it might even have been the decision to undertake the direction of such a project that was to fire Gaudí with the Christian ardor that until then had lain dormant in him, making of him a true ascetic who in the last years of his life was entirely detached from earthly concerns other than architecture. This development was certainly accelerated by the amount of time that he spent in the company of such eminent clergymen as Bishop Enrique d'Ossó and the Bishop of Astorga and also by some painful family experiences. It was in his early 40s that Gaudí declared: "A man without religion is a spiritually diminished man, a mutilated man."

Gaudí initially concentrated on building the crypt; this took four years, during which he carried out a complete and highly unorthodox revision of his predecessor's plans. In accordance with tradition, Villar had located the crypt beneath the apse, and had made it the same shape as the apse. Access to the crypt was provided by a stairway that was as wide as the nave. Gaudí did nothing less than turn the crypt in the opposite direction to the church, replacing the great stairway with five chapels, the central one of which was to contain the main altar. He also redesigned the pillars, increased the height of the crypt and had a ditch dug around it; this made it possible for the elevation of the new walls and the ribs of the vault to be seen from the outside. The plan for the building itself, which Gaudí's collaborator, the architect Joan Rubió i Bellver, finished drawing up in 1915, was not published until 1917. Its final form had, however, probably been decided at the beginning of the 1890s. This was to be a Latin cross consisting of a nave and four aisles, the nave to be 295 feet (90 meters) long, 49 feet (15 meters) wide and 148 feet (45 meters) high; an apse lined with chapels; and a transept 98 feet (30 meters) wide. A tower 558 feet (170 meters) high was to rise over the crossing.

The first known complete plan for the Sagrada Familia was not unveiled until April 1917, when it was published in the *Propagador de la Devoción de San José.* Twelve years later—three years after Gaudí's death—the final plan was devised on the basis

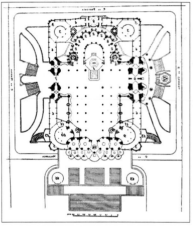

of Gaudí's last sketches and most particularly after the large model that had been created under his direction. This plan corresponds to the neo-Gothic model advocated by Viollet-le-Duc, but its dry, theoretical aspect was swallowed up by the forest of columns, the parabolic arches, and the breathtakingly lofty domes dedicated to Christ, the Virgin Mary and the Evangelists over the transept and presbytery.

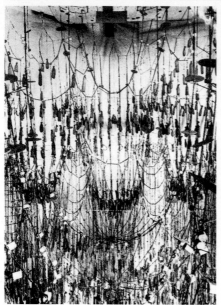 

A new architectural equilibrium

According to Joan Bergós, it took Gaudí about ten years to solve the problems posed by the erection of the nave walls. In order to formulate and perfect their structure, he used plaster models, some of which he turned upside down. This was in order to measure stresses by means of forces in suspension: those above were to equal those below. With his great admiration for the Gothic style, and his complete knowledge of its most minute detail, Gaudí aimed not to take his inspiration from it, as Villar had done, but to re-create its dynamism by means of forms and techniques that had never before been seen or used. This led him to take the bold and spectacular step of abandoning the buttresses and flying buttresses that would normally have supported the nave and prevented it from collapsing. "The traditional Gothic scheme," he said, "is a dead system. It might be compared to a human being whose skeleton, instead of enabling the different parts of the body to hang together harmoniously, is

Although Gaudí knew nothing of the theories of the 18th-century Italian physician Poleni, unknowingly he applied them when he made the model for the church in the Colonia Güell. Lengths of string traced the load lines of the vaults and the angle of the columns that would support them. Small bags of buckshot, representing the load to be borne, were suspended from the columns. It was from this model, known today only from a photograph by Vicente Villarubias, one of his assistants, that Gaudí made the wash drawing shown above.

crushed by the weight of flesh that it has to support, and needs crutches in every direction." With these intentions, it is not surprising that research and experiment on the columns took several years. The final result was that the external buttresses were replaced by tiered supports on the interior, which fulfilled the same function. The Gothic arches were replaced by parabolic arches resting on slanting columns, a combination that allowed the weight of the enormous vault to be borne. The consequence on the exterior was that the lateral facades were smoother and the bell towers could be set back, thus considerably accentuating the overall impression of verticality. The columns also display a spiral twist; unlike straight columns, which create a certain sense of inertia, these contribute to the dynamism of the whole.

In Gaudí's view, the ridges of the spiral "brought the column to life," forcing it "to stand up straighter and straighter, to awaken to itself, truly to live in its own right." The springing of the vault is marked by a clump from which the columns branch out like the boughs of a tree. The result is twofold: while, visually, the vaulting is extremely fragmented, from a technical point of view the columns bear the load more evenly. The impression created by the interior of the Sagrada Familia is very much that of a vast and imposing forest illuminated by a mysterious light—mysterious because its source is difficult to identify, but which in fact filters through the gaps between the columns.

The workshop where the models were made was located in the undercroft of the Sagrada Familia. The most spectacular was the great polychrome model that was shown in Paris in 1910 when Gaudí was invited to exhibit at the Salon de la Société des Beaux-Arts. The model shown above, made in 1925, is of one of the side aisles. It inevitably brings to mind Gaudí's description of the aisles as "Exactly like being in a forest." The columns are infused with a dynamism comparable to the life force that enables a tree to grow and gives equilibrium.

An abundance of statuary

Gaudí's design for the Sagrada Familia featured three facades: the Nativity Facade on the east side; the Glory

Facade on the south side; and the Passion Facade on the
west front. Each was to be pierced by a great portal
having three doorways and being crowned with four
belltowers grouped in two pairs. At the time of
Gaudí's death, only the Nativity Facade was completed,
apart from the finials of the towers that were finished
soon after by Gaudí's assistants. Facing northeast, the
facade is lit by the rising sun and symbolizes the mystery

of the Incarnation. The iconography focuses on the
birth and childhood of Christ; in the portal, the central
door is dedicated to Charity, that on the right to
Faith, and that on the left to Hope. The numerous
photographs taken at the time show precisely how
Gaudí set about creating the sculptures for the portals.
His procedure was skillful, empirical, ingenious, and
craftsmanlike, but it may seem excessively so in terms
of the sheer immensity of the work and the imperious
need for formal unity.

This procedure was based on photography (notably
an album of views taken between 1892 and 1900 and
compiled by one of Gaudí's assistants, the draftsman
Ricardo Opisso), casts taken from living and sometimes
dead people, plants, and objects, and also models
constructed in iron or brass, which were easy to handle
and certainly more compliant than a living model,
although Gaudí used them too.

In 1906, the groups
already in place on the
Nativity Facade (above)
were only plaster casts,
put up provisionally at
Gaudí's behest so that he
could judge the
distortions due to the
distance from the ground
and rectify them on the
final sculptures. In 1878
he wrote: "It is essential
to place the sculpture in
conditions where it is
clearly visible, otherwise
it is superfluous and
harmful to the whole."
Left: this drawing of the
Passion Facade was
found in Gaudí's pocket
on the day of his fatal
accident.

Gaudí's approach to sculpture was identical to that which he had to architecture; he proceeded by trial and error, and this could continue for a matter of years. On the site of the Sagrada Familia, where he had set up his office (see pages 86–87), he had a storeroom (shown on pages 88–89 in a photograph of 1917) where the casts for the portals were kept and meticulously numbered. Hanging from the ceiling was a particularly noticeable row of casts that Lorenzo Matamala had made from stillborn babies at the Santa Cruz maternity hospital. Casts of plants, animals, and live models were also made. The draftsman Ricardo Opisso, then aged 25, was called upon for the figure of one of the herald angels: "I stripped down to my trunks, and Gaudí insisted that I take up the pose he wanted. Then the sculptors Lorenzo Matamala and Ramón coated my body with plaster. But I soon had such a pain in the stomach that I fainted."

When one or other of these did not prove entirely satisfactory, or when there was a need to probe more deeply so as to obtain a satisfactory solution, the architect resorted to actual skeletons, which were obtained for him by the young Joan Matamala, the son of the sculptor Lorenzo Matamala, who was particularly involved in work on the Nativity portal. Such recourse was driven by the fact that the sculpture of the Sagrada Familia, like its architectural design, depended above all on structure. The aim of this titanic labor was not of course an exact reproduction of reality, but a perfect understanding of the hidden mechanisms and dynamics that are all but invisible.

Unfortunately, none of this material, which Gaudí's assistants scrupulously preserved after his death, is still in existence today. On 20 July 1936, during the Spanish Civil War, the workshops of the Sagrada Familia—where Gaudí, much affected by the deaths of relatives and

friends, had installed his bed and gone to live alone—were ransacked and burned. All the casts and the archives—except for the photographs, which were rescued in the nick of time by Joan Matamala—were destroyed. Many sculptures on the Nativity Facade were also damaged, the angels on the central archivolt in particular. The tomb in the crypt in which Gaudí had been buried on 12 June 1926 was desecrated, and it was only thanks to the vigilance of an astute Catalan member of the Guardia Civil that the mob was prevented from carrying out its intention to blow up the four towers with dynamite.

Financial difficulties

The fact that this gigantic construction could not be completed during Gaudí's lifetime was not perhaps due to lack of time so much as to lack of money. On several occasions the architect's friends expressed their outrage over the dearth of funds; in 1905, for example, Joan Maragall published four articles in the pages of the *Diaro de Barcelona*, in which he alluded very particularly

Thanks to Ricardo Opisso, Gaudí's recruitment of the models for the trumpeting angels on the columns of the Nativity Facade (right) is documented. Some young soldiers learning to blow their bugles disturbed Gaudí while he was holding a conversation with the Bishop of Barcelona. When he asked them to stop, they flew into a temper and refused. The prelate intervened, after which they calmed down and "Gaudí with his devilish shrewdness was able to persuade them to pose as the angels".

to the financial difficulties that the project faced: "I have very often felt as proud to be from Barcelona as an ancient Roman would have been of his citizenship; at other times, however, I am ashamed of it, and this is one of them. The man who is building the temple of the Sagrada Familia tells me that the resources for the continuation of this work are running out, and that donations are dwindling.... The temple of the Sagrada Familia is Barcelona's monument to the Catalan ideal, the monument to eternally ascending piety, the tangible expression in stone of the desire to rise up, the image of the popular soul.... The day when the building of the Sagrada Familia has to stop for lack of funds will be more disastrous for Barcelona and Catalunya than a bomb going off on the public highway, or the closure of a hundred factories."

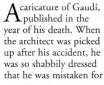

A caricature of Gaudí, published in the year of his death. When the architect was picked up after his accident, he was so shabbily dressed that he was mistaken for a tramp.

Despite the subsidies that Gaudí himself obtained by literally begging for charity and pursuing his contacts—who would sometimes cross the street when they saw him coming—the deficit had risen to 30,000 pesetas just before World War I. The project was then seriously threatened by the disruption of the war, and the number of workmen reduced to six or seven.

The commission in charge of the construction of the temple, which had been set up in 1895 by the

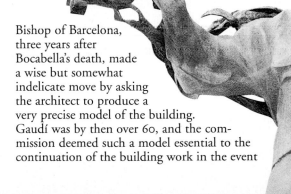

Bishop of Barcelona, three years after Bocabella's death, made a wise but somewhat indelicate move by asking the architect to produce a very precise model of the building. Gaudí was by then over 60, and the commission deemed such a model essential to the continuation of the building work in the event

of the master's death. This model, comprising the
apse, the vault over the nave, the sacristies, the entire
Nativity Facade, and the upper part of the Glory
Facade, was destroyed in the fire of 1936. Work resumed
after the Civil War, but progress was very slow, again
for financial reasons. Since 1985 it has been speeded up
by the appointment of the architect Jordi Bonet as head
of the project and in 1986, amid some controversy,
Josep Maria Subirachs created a sculptural group for
the Passion Facade. While work continues to complete
the building in as faithful a way as possible, there have
been calls for it to stop so that this unique and
extraordinary building be left to stand unfinished as a
memorial to Gaudí.

"He never used a single element more than once" (Ricardo Bofill)

As the construction of the Sagrada Familia continued
throughout Gaudí's life, it is hard to resist drawing
parallels between the development of this project and
the other buildings that he designed. Some specialists
hold that everything that Gaudí undertook besides the
Sagrada Familia was governed by the intention of
producing and testing solutions to the problems posed
by the cathedral; although this may be going too far,
there is no doubt that there are numerous points of
overlap between the cathedral and his other commissions. Suffice it to give two examples, neither of
which has yet been mentioned. The first is the church in
the Colonia Güell, of which only the crypt was built.
The second, which never got beyond the planning stage,
was a hotel in New York.

In 1890, Eusebi Güell had built a velvet factory on
his property in Santa Colonna de Cervelló, a few miles
west of Barcelona. Around this he created a village,
which in 1892 became officially known as the Colonia
Güell and which housed about 1,000 families. In 1898
Güell commissioned Gaudí to build a church for
this workers' estate, which at the time of his death
in 1918 was still incomplete. For this project the
architect, assisted by his assistant Francesc Berenguer
(1866–1914)—on whose death Gaudí declared that he

This aerial view, taken
in the early 1920s,
gives a clear idea of the
sheer size of the Sagrada
Familia. Its dimensions
clearly show the extent to
which the building was
linked to the theme of
the sacred mountain and
the mountain of miracles.
Fleeing from an outbreak
of typhus in 1870,
Barcelonans, including
Bocabella, took refuge on
Montserrat, where there
was a shrine to the
Virgin. The common
identity that developed
between temple and
mountain was explored
by the poet Maragall in
Oda Nova a Barcelona,
written in 1910.

After the fire of July 1936 (below), the architect Bonet i Gari was given a labor force by the municipal services to reassemble the pieces of the plaster models that were stored in the workshop. At the end of the Civil War, the reconstruction of the crypt was begun—thanks to the million pesetas that had been deposited in a London bank before the events at the suggestion of Eusebi Güell's grandson Bertan—under the direction of Francesc de P. Quintara, who became Gaudí's successor after Domènec Sugranes died of despair in 1938. Religious services are still celebrated in the crypt today.

had lost his right arm—spent ten years developing a remarkable model. The lines of the vaulting and the cupolas and the angle of the slanting pillars were indicated by lengths of string, and small sacks filled with buckshot were suspended from strings to represent the weight of the load that would need to be supported. The aim was to solve the problem of parabolic arches bearing down without interruption on slanting columns. This model, made in the workshops of the Sagrada Familia, was used only for the construction of the crypt. The latter has a single central brick vault supported by four slanting basalt columns and a wall that fulfill the function of an apse. Around it is a

U-shaped ambulatory following the plan of the apse and opening on to the outside. It is composed of 11 slanting columns of varying forms and textures, whose arrangement may appear random but which blend into the surrounding pine forest. It was this building that gave Gaudí the opportunity to solve the technical problems associated with the parabolic arches that he wanted to use in the interior of the Sagrada Familia.

The surviving plans of the hotel that two New York financiers commissioned Gaudí to build in 1908 indicate that this design was also to be similar to that of the crypt of the Colonia Güell church. They show the same undulating forms as those of Casa Milá, and the same parabolic verticality as that of the belltowers of the Sagrada Familia. It was intended that this prestigious hotel should be set in gardens, with a location outside Manhattan, and that it should be visible from a great distance.

Gaudí imagined a building reaching a height of 1,016 feet (310 meters)—a little higher than the Eiffel Tower and not quite as high as the Empire State Building of some 20 years later. The main tower and the 11 towers surrounding it all had parabolic outlines.

They were to be clad in marble of various colors, and some of the side towers were to have had cladding similar to that of Casa Milá. Had Gaudí traveled to New York to supervise the construction of this vast building in person, he would doubtless have improvised and come to terms with the unyielding metal elements of American architecture that his patrons had insisted be

The surviving drawing of the church for the Colonia Güell (above) shows a building that is located not at the center of the village as places of worship traditionally are, but on a hill overlooking the small estate. It was to be reached by a path and a bridge with a single parabolic arch. On account of its dimensions, more than simply satisfying the spiritual needs of the population, the church could also be a meeting place. Its several elongated domes, grouped around a central dome and covered with ceramics in intense colors, would have given it pride of place in the architectural hierarchy of the village, and supremacy over the nearby industrial buildings. Left, one of the projects for the great New York hotel.

used. Probably for health reasons, he never made the journey to the United States.

This project nevertheless helped Gaudí to create the final models for the Sagrada Familia, in the same way that he had benefited from the experiments that he had tirelessly carried out over more than 20 years on this sublime construction, for which there is perhaps no equivalent in the history of architecture. The titanic inspiration with which it is infused is closer to that of epic literature; it could be said that the Sagrada Familia suggests a visionary epic combining the myths of the

The apertures on the sides of the crypt of the Colonia Güell church are fitted with brightly colored stained-glass windows, some in the shape of rose windows, others decorated with a cross. On the outside these windows have a border of *trencadís*, whose sparkling texture harmonizes with that of the stained glass.

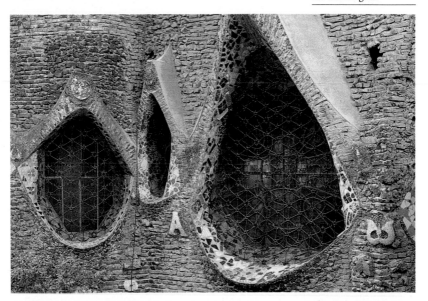

ancient world with the marvels of Christianity. This fusion was, it seems, what the architect was seeking to achieve, given that he described his work as the "Hellenic temple of Mediterranean Gothic."

On several occasions Gaudí declared that his death must in no way interrupt the construction of the Sagrada Familia. Even as the architect is being accorded beatification in Rome, work on the cathedral continues to this day (see page 96).

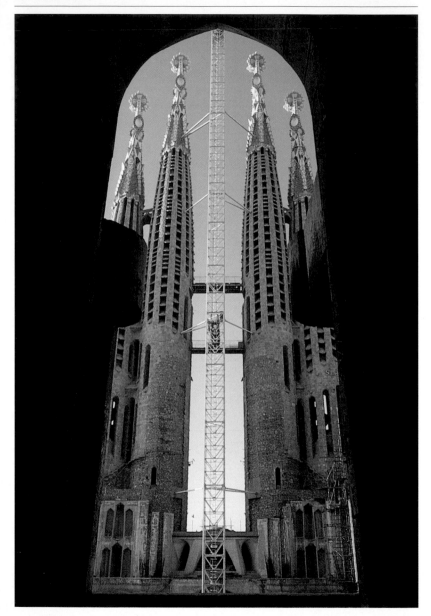

DOCUMENTS

Differing interpretations

During Gaudí's lifetime his work was studied and judged only by his compatriots. Despite the abundance and high quality of the art journals in existence at the time, it was virtually ignored by critics in other countries. As a result, the exhibition devoted to Gaudí in 1910 by the Salon de la Société des Beaux-Arts in Paris provoked hardly any interested reactions, and no foreign architect thought of making the journey to Barcelona for a firsthand experience of the master's creations.

The philosopher and architect

Francesc Pujols (Barcelona 1882– Martorell 1962) was a Catalan intellectual and the creator of a philosophical system known as the Pantologia. In 1927 he wrote an essay on Gaudí suggesting an esoteric reading of his work which in general was refuted by the architect's disciples.

THE GREAT ORGANS OF BARCELONA

This great architectural constructor has quite rightly been described as the poet of stone; one might also call him a musician—and not only a musician of the silence that accompanies architecture, and of the wind that cuts in a very original way through the groins of the stones and walls and sings with very different sonorities from those of the buildings of the other modern architects contemporary with Gaudí who are elderly or deceased. He is also a musician because he told us that he had devised a general system of tubular bells operated by a keyboard which would ring out in all the bell towers of the temple, fifteen or twenty of them creating melodies and harmonies which would be heard throughout Barcelona in the morning, at noon and in the evening. He could also be regarded as a sculptor of architecture who, not content with introducing numerous figures from the organic world—a world that belongs to the realm of sculpture as the inorganic world belongs to that of architecture, gave an organic quality to the conception of both the whole and the detail of the buildings that he constructed, especially the most recent ones. We might also call him a painter, not only thanks to his design for an entirely polychrome temple, but also because of the buildings where, as we all know, he produced decorative combinations of color, achieving effects of the greatest purity and finesse that melt beneath our eyes and gaze like sugar in the mouth. He was also an architect who esteemed and adored Greek art throughout his life as few others have done, and who has left us a building like the Sagrada Familia, of which it was said one day by a cabby— guiding his cabhorse with reins and whip in hand and turning to the visitor he was taking to the temple, who was sitting inside the stationary cab staring

Idealized axonometric drawing of the Church of the Sagrada Familia, by Fransisco Valles.

at this sublime fragment of Gaudí's cathedral—that this facade was made entirely from stones that were chipped away by hand, with a hammer. This is something that we ourselves have heard during one of the frequent visits we have made, still make and will continue to make to the fragmentary facade of this temple, which may never be finished and which makes silence sing out in the Campo de l'Arpa where this modern temple stands. In a language both concrete and symbolic, Gaudí called this facade the Door of Life or Door of Birth; there are cocks and hens there, as at a farm gate. The other lateral facade on the opposite side was to be the Door of Death, and the main portal of the temple would be the Door of Resurrection. Gaudí explained them to us and made us see them as clearly as if they were already finished. It was almost as if one could go in and out of them, because—as we have said and will repeat so as to sum up the artistic vision that we have just communicated before passing on to the religious vision which we are about to communicate— he was a man who possessed every faculty, and when he had thought of something it was as if he had already executed it.

THE INHERENT POWER OF ART NOUVEAU

In any case, we will leave aside our own style—which is never essentially anything other than propaganda, something full of that pious insistence that was recommended a few years ago by the admirable Eugenio d'Ors. We will favor instead our scientific ideas and basic Catalonian ideals, we shall say with regard to Gaudí's style that, although it is obvious that a city built according to his conception of architecture, that is built on the basis of his monstrous, baroque and contorted grand style, would have been an equally monstrous, baroque and contorted city with monstrous, baroque, contorted streets, squares, buildings and gardens like Güell Park, Casa Milá and the Sagrada Familia. It is also obvious that it would have been the most aesthetically vibrant of all modern cities, which, as we all know, are cities of this scientific age, being constructed mechanically and mathematically like a work of science, with no aesthetic consideration other than academicism. To those who tell us that a "Gaudian" city would have been horrible and exorbitant, and who are already prepared to close their eyes in order not to see the artistic vision that this might suggest, we shall reply that we do not know why they should be astonished by a modern city contorting and deforming its architecture in order to rekindle the living, flamboyant essence of fundamental aesthetic emotion, and this precisely in these modern times which, as we all know, have contorted poetry, music, painting and sculpture in order to reveal the aesthetic element already mentioned, which we have lost in the cold, correct application of academic canons, leaving architecture to Gaudí as if we wanted this architect to take sole responsibility for doing in architecture what had already been done collectively and successfully in the four other arts.

If in the time of Wagner and Cézanne, who contorted the musical and pictorial visions that they had, respectively breaking the canons of music and Italian painting, in the time of Strauss and Stravinsky in music and of Picasso in painting, not to mention their followers and imitators in poetry and sculpture—which in this movement and its tendencies are two art forms which did not take the initiative in deforming the canons, but limited themselves to following the lessons and practical examples of music and painting, which were the first to launch out into the artistic adventure of modern times—if then at a time like this we do not find it very natural and rational that a city should exist such as the one that Gaudí would have designed and constructed if he had been allowed to, it is as if we did not find it natural that it should exist in

the middle of a period of primitive civilization, when art produced the deformations and monstrosities that we know and have seen all through the history of art in the ardent productions of primitive peoples, who no doubt, as we claim, created this style in their own way because they did not know any better, but who, because of this, as in the paintings, drawings and writings of our children today when they are still at the age of innocence, gain from this primitive deformation born of difficulties and ignorance a quantity of very powerful, vital aesthetic expression, that same quantity and quality which artists seek today when they break everything up, without pity or compassion for the whole, twisting and deforming whatever suits them, and above all knowing that this artistic conception will not appeal to most, but will provoke deep reactions in people, as all artistic contortionists know who think only of the sensitive minority who are capable of attaining the keen emotion that they are looking for and want to find and give, some in a grandiose way like Wagner, Cézanne and Gaudí, who as Homeric creators and deformers destroy the sublime harmony of that great Greek poet Homer, the greatest Classical poet who ever existed or ever will exist, and seize hold of his grandeur and grace, others in a very delicate fashion, as if they were painting or writing with insects' horns which are the antennae that test out reality as the organs of human sensibility must test out the artistic visions that affect the soul.

Wagner, Strauss and Stravinsky sought new forms of music by return-ing to the primitive conception of art by means of a most acute refinement which is close to the primitive state in that it brings together the extremes. When Wagner was deforming the established structure of Italian music, Strauss was increasing the ambits of stridency and sonoritiy. Stravinsky was shrilly breaking up melodies and harmonies so as to reach through to the guts. Cézanne was deforming faces and landscapes so that he could intensify pictorial vision, and Picasso was doing the same and triumphing in Paris with his inspired, feline skills after spending the early years of his life in Barcelona, where his parents lived even though they were not Catalans. During all that time, Gaudí, as silent as stone, saying nothing, was doing likewise, obeying the same rhythm of the modern revolutionary artistic tragedy and returning to the fundamental principles of all peoples. He did this without budging from Barcelona and without knowing Wagner or Strauss or Stravinsky or Cézanne, or even Picasso, or anyone else, in the same way as they did not know him or know who he was; thus Gaudí, and therefore Catalonia, were doing as others were doing, and without budging from Barcelona or displaying themselves in the international marketplace of modern art, were participating in the artistic fever of our time, in the one art form that other countries had neglected or subjected to the classical canons of Antiquity and the necessities of modern construction, which twists iron like straw and makes stones out of the cement that was previously used to link and join stones together.

In conclusion to these thoughts on the history of art and its characteristics in modern times, we may add that Wagner, Cézanne and the other revolutionary innovators who sought a living aesthetic tradition founded on palpable emotion were operating on the backs of a multitude of other artists whose slow innovations had prepared day by day for the artistic revolution of the 19th and 20th centuries. This revolution was a resounding triumph of aesthetic essence over the canonical debris of pure forms which had lost all life in those eminently scientific times; then, the greenest leaves on the artistic tree had dried up, since the wind of science was hardly favorable to aesthetic revolt, and it took the enlightened modern sensibility of this same age, the most scientific ever known, to rebuild the essential vision of the work of art. Gaudí, on the other hand, unlike Wagner, Cézanne and the others, began the revolution all on his own in Barcelona, without precedents either here or elsewhere, because the modern styles that he followed and imitated, just as he followed those of ancient times, were not styles that fought for the aesthetic essence we have talked about here, which was the supreme aspiration of a 19th- and 20th-century sensibility based on irritation with the scientific death of the work of art. Thus as we place Catalonia in the history of art as we might place it on a map, we find Gaudí doing with his genius alone everything that other geniuses in other countries and other branches of art did by summing up and perfecting the efforts of the artists who had gone before them.

Francesc Pujols
La Visió artística i religiosa
d'En Gaudí (Gaudí's Artistic
and Religious Vision)
Barcelona, 1927

The vision of a poet

Between 1910 and 1914, the French poet Guillaume Apollinaire expressed two very different visions of Gaudí.

The architecture section has mounted a general exhibition of the Catalan architect Gaudí. Let us hope that our architects do not take inspiration from his fantasies.

Decorative art here, which should be one of the chief concerns of the Société Nationale des Beaux-Arts, is frankly bad.

Guillaume Apollinaire
L'Intransigeant, 19 April 1910

Antoni Gaudí is a Catalan architect whose buildings have transformed Barcelona. He is one of the most personal of modern architects. Among other things, he has brought to a very high point the art of the terrace and everything that is found on the roofs of houses, thus giving the city that tumultuous, animated appearance that most of what we call modern construction did away with.

The Milá house is one of the most complete and pleasing works he has produced.

It would be useful if this architect became known here. The Salon d'Automne, whose next exhibition will feature the greatest Viennese architect, ought also to introduce us to Antoni Gaudí and the Catalan architects, as well as to Czech architects and those of the American skyscrapers, who I believe studied at the Ecole des Beaux-Arts. They have put to good use the teaching they received here, and it is only right that we should get to know them.

Guillaume Apollinaire
L'Intransigeant, 14 July 1914

An intransigent press at the 1910 Salon

The number of models exhibited by M. Gaudé (Antoni) of Barcelona is frightening; there are models on a small scale and others on a larger scale, not to mention a vast number of photographs of his numerous works. There is certainly not a Frenchman among us who has built so much. What is perhaps uncertain, however, is that all of it is indeed architecture! We will even venture to say that, apart from a few fragmentary sketches that are in fact quite inaccurate, and some working drawings that would have you believe the buildings they depict are stable, we did not see a single architect's plan or drawing, just models and photographs…

Most of Gaudé's works are exhibited in a special room lit by electricity and closed off by a large curtain. One is immediately reminded of those little closed-off rooms at fairgrounds to which only men are admitted and entry to which is gained in exchange for a small extra charge.

Fortunately, at the [Société] Nationale there is no extra charge for admittance to this special room devoted to M. Gaudé (Antoni), but although what is to be seen in there is in no way obscene, there is nothing very beautiful about it either! One wonders how anyone can build an edifice like this "Sagrada Familia" temple in Barcelona, whose facade is represented here by an enormous, highly colored model. And yet, if one might doubt the existence of this building, that doubt would be dispelled by photographs showing it under construction. Is this something from Dahomey [Benin]? Not even! At most it is the architecture of the confectioner and ice-cream-maker. One can imagine this extraordinary tiered cake appearing on Gargantua's table. I wouldn't like to taste it, however! I find those colors most offputting!

J. Godefroy, in *L'Architecture*
Société Nationale des Beaux-Arts
7 July 1910

A tribute by Le Corbusier

During a trip to Spain in the spring of 1928 the French architect Le Corbusier (1887–1965) discovered the work of Gaudí, as can be seen from a drawing that he made of the parish school of the Sagrada Familia.

We were going to Sitjes; on the road, I was intrigued by a modern house. Gaudí. And on the way back, at the Paseo de Grácia, my attention was seized by some large apartment blocks; farther on was the Sagrada Familia. The whole Gaudí story was unfolding!

I was sufficiently relaxed to show a lively interest in it, because I saw in it the emotional essence of 1900. That was the year when I was opening my eyes to artistic things, and I have always looked back on it with great affection.

Coming from me—the "soapbox" architect of the La Roche and Garches houses and the Villa Savoye—my friends found this attitude disconcerting.

Is there an antagonism between 1900 and the "soapbox"? I did not even ask myself the question. What there was in Barcelona—Gaudí—was the work of a man whose extraordinary strength, faith and technical capacity manifested themselves throughout a lifetime of building, a man who was there to watch as the stones were cut according to his truly scholarly working drawings. Gaudí was "the builder" of "1900", a working professional, a builder in stones, iron and brick. His glory is apparent now in his own country. Gaudí was a great

A bove: the schools built by Gaudí in the Sagrada Familia close in 1909–10; the walls and roofs are designed as a continuous, sinuous entity. Below: a sketch by Le Corbusier, whose interest in Gaudí's work was stimulated when he visited Barcelona in 1928.

artist; only those who touch the emotional hearts of men live on and will continue to do so. Yet along the way they will be roughly handled, misunderstood or accused of sinning according to the fashion of the day. The meaning of this architecture bursts forth when higher intentions triumph, gaining the upper hand over all the problems that architects would like to be rid of (problems of structure, economics, technology, utility). They triumph thanks to endless inner preparation: this architecture is the fruit of spirit, or more precisely the manifestation of spirit.

Le Corbusier
From the preface (1957)
to *Gaudí* (1967)

The Surrealist tribute

Gaudí's architecture eschews pure geometry and exhibits a close affinity with living and natural forms that stimulate the imagination. It is not surprising, therefore, that it was the Surrealists who were responsible for the architect's initial return to critical favor.

In December 1933, seven years after Gaudí's death, the newly founded periodical *Minotaure* published Salvador Dalí's famous article entitled "On the Terrifying and Edible Beauty of Modern Architectural Style." Despite its generic title, the article is actually a vibrant tribute to the work of two architects: Hector Guimard and Antoni Gaudí.

It was to Man Ray (1890–1976) that Dalí, on the advice of Marcel Duchamp, turned to provide the photographs that would illustrate his argument. But there is absolutely nothing documentary about Man Ray's photographs of Park Güell, Casa Battló and Casa Milá. The details that he chose and the lighting and angle of the shots betray a subjective approach that had previously been very rare in the specialized field of architectural photography. The images speak the same language as the text to such an extent that it is difficult to place the one above the other as an expression of Surrealist thinking. The photographer's vision may have determined the way in which Dalí wrote the captions to the photographs. They have a flavorsome character. This is how Dalí commented on the image of the doorway of a portico: "One enters the grottoes through soft, calf's-liver doors," while the interior of the portico is described as a "mammoth super-neurosis," and the *trencadís* bench on the terrace is presented as the expression of

"the extra-fine, undulating, polychrome, guttural neurosis." To Dalí's eyes, the facade of Casa Milá suggested "the fossilized waves of the sea," and one of its balconies "foaming wrought-iron." As for Casa Battló, its bones were on the outside. These pages from *Minotaure* are among the most valuable pieces of evidence showing the link between Art Nouveau and Surrealism.

Dalí came to regard as perfectly well-founded the comparison so often made by Gaudí's detractors between his art and that of the confectioner and the ice-cream-maker: "I repeat that this is lucid and intelligent comparison, not only because it exposes a violent materialist-mundanity of immediate, urgent need, on which ideal desires are based, but also because, by that very fact and in reality, it alludes without euphemism to the nutritious, edible character of houses like this, which are nothing other than the first and only houses that can be eroticized, and whose existence verifies this urgent 'function' that is so necessary to the imagination of someone in love: the ability in as real a way as possible to eat the object of desire." Gaudí's re-creation of elusive natural elements in perpetual motion—Dalí saw Casa Milá as "a house following the forms of the sea and showing the waves on a stormy day"—is certainly an invitation to reverie, but also to consumption.

Casa Battló was described by Dalí as "a real sculpture of the reflections of twilight clouds on water, made possible by using a vast, bizarre, multicolored, gleaming mosaic, Pointillist iridescences from which emerge forms of water spilled out, forms of water splilling out, forms of stagnant water, forms of shimmering water, forms of water rippling in the wind, all these forms of water constructed in an asymmetrical, dynamic-instantaneous succession of broken, syncopated, interlaced reliefs that are fused together by 'naturalist-stylized' water lilies materializing in eccentric, impure, destructive convergences, in thick protruberances of fear, springing out from the incredible facade, contorted by all the suffering of insanity and at the same time by a latent, infinitely gentle calm equalled only by that of the horrifying, glorious fungal growths, ripe and ready to eat with a spoon."

For Dalí, Gaudí's architecture was not merely in harmony with the Surrealist avant-garde. He saw it both as a tool and as one of the most beautiful products of the paranoid-critical method. In addition, however, it represented a weapon in the battle against the functionalist architecture of his time.

Dalí's article in *Minotaure* had been intended mainly as a response to the attack launched against Gaudí in the *Cahiers d'Art* (Art Journals), which favored "ultra-modern" architecture. Many years later, he told of the satisfaction that he had felt when he saw Clovis Prévost's photographs: they were, he said "more anti–Le Corbusier than anything that would most have disgusted the Protestant Corbu." Nor did he resist taking malicious pleasure in recalling the declaration made to him in 1929 by Le Corbusier that Gaudí was

Salvador Dalí seen against the halo of a ceiling medallion in the great columned hall at Güell Park.

"the manifest shame of Barcelona." His merciless retort was that "the last great genius of architecture was called Gaudí, which in Catalan means 'pleasure,' just as 'Dalí' means 'desire,'" and he explained that "pleasure and desire are the distinctive features of Mediterrean Catholicism and Gothic, and were brought to paroxysm by Gaudí."

Whether or not one adheres to it, the Surrealist interpretation of Gaudian architecture clearly makes a highly interesting contribution to the understanding of the Surrealist movement itself, and also explains why, up until the end of the 1950s, modern architectural historians found it so difficult to place within architectural history in general and that of Art Nouveau in particular. Its profound originality was hard to rediscover: it was easier to ignore it and regard it as the work of a visionary or a crank.

Philippe Thiébaut

"A notorious landmark"

This article published in the architectural journal The Builder *in 1927 expresses the bewilderment and lack of understanding that the originality and novelty of Gaudí's style inspired up until the 1950s.*

The south front [of the church of the Sagrada Familia] needs a preparation of the mind before it can be appreciated. It has been called "unhealthy," "debased," "the worst architecture ever." The porches raise doubts as to being architecture at all; for the structural lines are lost almost everywhere, and only occasionally are seen, merely sketched in, through a smother of foliage, texts and figures, stars and grotto work. Practically the whole porches are carved, and if they had no structure above, might be judged as a sculpture. The great spires make that impossible, and the mind rushes to any similar work, however remote the affiliation, the thought of which will relieve the feeling of strangeness and make this amazing *tour de force* human and familiar. For mere richness there is the memory of Rheims [cathedra], or the west entrance to Toledo [cathedral], where an Englishman is startled by a presentation of the Christ with Shavian smile and beard. At Toledo, though, there are structural lines evident and representative of the weight carried by the wall, and the sculpture is enclosed by them. In Spain

Above: an "architectonic project" by Salvador Dalí dating from the time when the painter was discovering and interpreting Gaudí's work. The theme of the omnipresent eye is found again in the dreams of Dalí's amnesiac hero, who appears in Alfred Hitchcock's movie *Spellbound.* Gaudí's architecture was used as the setting for *Salomé,* a movie based on the work by Oscar Wilde and shot in 1969 by Pierre Koralnik. It also featured in Michelangelo Antonioni's movie *Profession: Reporter* of 1975.

the inspiration for sculptured figures still comes from a religious reaction of Christendom against Islam. Granada fell but a generation before the English Reformation, of which the prejudices are still current here. The Moor forbade by the tenets of his religion all illusions of natural objects....

Certainly Gaudí had adopted the principle [of using sculpted figures— "incarnate stone" structurally] itself in these south porches, and throughout the work has never forgotten it. The porches are devoted to the Nativity of Jesus, and the subject is thrust upon the spectator; the story is told to the last half inch, the structural lines of the building are all but suppressed, as though the true reserve in this case were the reservation of the whole stage for the drama of the birth and boyhood of Christ. The very

Old photograph of the roofs of Casa Milá.

columns and caps represent palm trunks and branches of Palestine and Egypt.

The spires, probably like all successful spires, are contained within a parabola. These four of the south front follow an actual parabolic line. The piercings indicate the spiral ascents within; but the great number of openings gives a somewhat all-overish effect, even from a distance; like an American sky-scraper. The one finished spire has an enormous finial, built up of stone faceted to catch the light, and covered with coloured Venetian glass mosaic, which sparkles in the sun. There is a look of distortion about the upper portion of the finial as of a vertebrate thing holding itself upright with difficulty; at the top is a flattened round shape, spread like a sunflower, and framed with glass beads. The natural bizarrerie is increased by the newness; it reminds one of a garish and *outré* electric sign. When it becomes dirty and its rawness is covered with grime, the appearance may be rich and not unbecoming to this exotic sky. The central spire actually is to have a cross to be lit up at night by electric light. Probably Gaudí knew what he was doing, though no one else will, until the whole forest of spires grows up.

The Englishman feels himself on surer ground beneath the archway into the cloisters. Here, too, is dramatic effect, but all obtained by familiar means, and with architectural technique. The flexibility of Gothic may astonish those who have forgotten it, the depth of carving may seem excessive until the blessed shade of Grinling Gibbons whispers assurance. No one can disregard the composition, rich intellectual, dramatic.

P̶hotographic montage by Robert Descharnes combining an image of Salvador Dalí on the rocks at Cap Creus with a detail of the sculpture on the Nativity Facade of the Sagrada Familia.

The portion of the church already built is now a notorious landmark. The Catalonian workman knows it and likes it, watches the slow movement of the scaffolding about it which keeps it alive, and picnics in its one completed porch, humorously regarding the carved beasts and birds and men, and the quixotic glances of the spires.

P. M. Stratton, "The Sagrada Familia (Holy Family) Church, Barcelona" *The Builder*, 5 August 1927

"A violent and delightful shock"

By the 1950s Gaudí's work had begun to receive greater appreciation and critical understanding. In the informal context of a talk broadcast by the BBC, the architecture historian Nikolaus Pevsner (1902–83) describes Gaudí as "unique" and "the most inimitable of architects."

Altogether … it is his treatment of materials and surfaces that makes him unique in his age. I say unique and mean unique. So far I have spoken of him mostly as a giant of Art Nouveau; now we must look at him as a man of the twentieth century, the direct predecessor of that other great Spaniard, Picasso. For you must not forget that Picasso grew up with Gaudí. Picasso left Barcelona for good only in 1903. So he must have watched that very change in Gaudí's style which concerns us here. And if I tell you a little more of Gaudí's use of ceramics you will no doubt realise what I mean. Take this, for instance. The market hall has between its Doric columns little vaults high up. They are there to give glitter, and so he has faced them with pottery and glass. But when you look up steadily and screw up your eyes a bit, you suddenly discern that that white disc up there is a cheap saucer, and that green, boldly modelled disc the bottom of a broken old bottle; and then, looking round the other vaults anxiously, you see necks of bottles sticking out, and cups with their handles, *collages* of before the First World War. It is a violent and a delightful shock, for the eyes as much as the mind.

One more word. Gaudí died in 1927, and since then the Barcelonese have pondered over the problem of what to do with the Sagrada Familia. I told you—no more is up, so far, than about one-eighth. What can be done? It is obvious to me that one cannot, even with all the dedicated lunacy of Spain, continue *a la Gaudí*. He was, you will now agree, the most personal, inimitable of architects. He kept only the fewest of designs or models. Every detail was decided face to face with the block and the surface. So there seem to me only two possible answers, one more tempting, the other probably more constructive. You can leave this cliff of a church as a ruin, plant the rest of the site sensitively, and enjoy the building in future as the hugest of all *custodias*—that is the Spanish name for those tower-shaped monstrances you see in the cathedrals. Or you can trust in the Spanish genius and make a competition inviting designs not in the style of Gaudí nor in the so-called international modern style. Perhaps amongst the talented young architects of Spain one would come forward, as fervent as Gaudí, and as original as he.

Nikolaus Pevsner
"The Strange Architecture of Antonio Gaudí"
The Listener
7 August 1952

Glory and delight

Coming to Barcelona just five years after Gaudí's death, the English novelist Evelyn Waugh (1903–66) made an almost accidental acquaintance with his work. He expresses surprise at Gaudí's secular buildings and marvels at the vast, still unfinished Sagrada Familia.

But the glory and delight of Barcelona, which no other town in the world can offer, is the architecture of Gaudí.... In England we scarcely know the meaning of *Art Nouveau*.... But this was not the case with the Catalans, who responded to the movement with all the zeal of their exuberant...nature. They never concerned themselves with Decadence or with archaism. *Art Nouveau* came to them at a time of commercial expansion and political unrest, and they took it to themselves and made it their own.... There are examples of it sparkling and blazing all over Barcelona, but Gaudí alone was able to use it with precision and enterprise and make of it the craft which, in New York, is reverently known as "Tiffany bathroom...."

[Waugh goes on to speak disparagingly of other Art Nouveau architects.] Gaudí bears to these anonymous contractors and job-builders something of the same relation as do the masters of Italian baroque to the rococo decorators of the Pompadours' boudoir, or Ronald Firbank to the author of *Frolic Wind*. What in them is frivolous, superficial and chic is in him structural and essential; in his work is apotheosized all the writhing, bubbling, convoluting, convulsing soul of *Art Nouveau*.

I could discover very little about his life save that it began in Barcelona, was for the most part spent there, and ended less than five years ago, when the aged and partially infirm master was run down and killed by an electric tramcar in the main boulevard of the town. In his later years he did very little creative work, devoting his failing energies to supervising the construction of the Great Church of the Holy Family.... The period of his grossest and wildest output is the last two decades of the last century; it was then that his art, cautiously maturing, broke through all preconceived bounds of order and propriety, and coursed wantonly over the town, spattering its riches on all sides like mud.

But, indeed, in one's first brush with Gaudí's genius, it is not so much propriety that is outraged as one's sense of probability. My interest in him began on the morning of my second and, unfortunately, my last day in Barcelona. I was walking alone and without any clear intention in my mind, down one of the boulevards, when I saw what, at first, I took to be part of the advertising campaign of the exhibition. On closer inspection I realized that it was a permanent building which, to my surprise, turned out to be the offices of the Turkish Consulate. Trees were planted in front of it along the pavement, hiding the lower storeys. It was the roof which chiefly attracted my attention; this was coloured peacock blue and built in undulations like a rough sea petrified; the

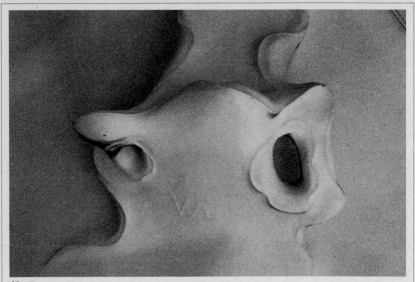

"Out of the ceilings come tadpoles bearing Ave Marias" (Casa Milá, 1963).

chimneys, too, were of highly coloured, glazed earthenware, and they were twisted and bent in all directions like very gnarled fruit trees. The front of the building, down to the level of the second row of windows, was made of the mosaic of broken china I have already described, but thoughtfully planned so that the colours merged in delicate gradations from violet to blue to peacock green and gold. The eaves overhung in irregular, amorphous waves, in places attenuated into stalactites of coloured porcelain, the effect being that of a clumsily iced cake. I cannot describe it more accurately than that because, dazzled and blinded by what I subsequently saw, my impression of this first experience, though deep, is somewhat indistinct. I went all round it with a camera trying to find an aspect I could photograph, but the trees and sun combined to frustrate me.

I knew now what I wanted to see in Barcelona.... I wanted to go to any other building like this one....

The whole of Gaudí's secular architecture seems to me summarized in [the Park Güell and the Sagrada Familia] and as I looked at them I could not help being struck by the kinship they bore to the settings of many of the later U.F.A. films. The dream scene in *Secrets of the Soul*, the Oriental passages in *Waxworks* particularly seem to me to show just the same inarticulate fantasy.

Only a small part has as yet been built of the great Church of the Holy Family, which was to have been Gaudí's supreme achievement, and unless some eccentric millionaire is moved to interpose in the near future, in spite of the great sums that have already been squandered upon it, the project will have to be abandoned.

The vast undertaking was begun with very small funds and relied entirely upon voluntary contributions for its progress. The fact that it has got as advanced as it has, is a testimony to the great enthusiasm it has aroused among the people of the country, but enthusiasm and contributions have dwindled during the last twenty years, until only ten men are regularly employed, most of their time being taken up in repairing the damage caused to the fabric by its exposure. There are already menacing cracks in the masonry; immense sums would be required to finish the building on the scale in which it was planned and the portions already constructed fatally compromise any attempt at modification. It seems to me certain that it will always remain a ruin, and a highly dangerous one, unless the towers are removed before they fall down....

I could easily have employed a happy fortnight at Barcelona tracking down further examples of Gaudism. He designed many things besides houses..., making it his special province to conceive designs for tables and chairs and other objects of common utility which rendered them wholly unfit for their ostensible purposes. He is a great example, it seems to me, of what Art for Art's sake can become when it is wholly untempered by considerations of tradition or good taste. Picabia in Paris is another example, but I think it would be more exciting to collect Gaudís.

Evelyn Waugh
"Gaudí," *The Architectural Review*
June 1930

P revious pages: *Starry Night over Bethlehem on the Portal of Charity,* Sagrada Familia, 1963.
Right: another view of the Sagrada Familia.

Gaudí's legacy

In this extract from his monograph on Gaudí, the American architecture historian George R. Collins paints a psychological portrait of Gaudí, describing his theories and attitudes, his working methods and his relationship with his many collaborators. The author concludes with an evaluation of Gaudí's impact on his contemporaries and, after a period of relative neglect, on later generations of artists and architects, from the American Abstract Expressionists of the 1940s and 1950s to architects of the present day.

Gaudí did not leave us an explicit architectural theory. He apparently never delivered a lecture nor wrote an article or book. What we have instead is a collection of dictums handed on to us by his associates, by visitors or by the press. These have been collected and published like the sayings of an Oriental holy man, a great deal of literature having been devoted to their exegesis. Some of his remarks are so cryptic as to have been explained variously: "Originalidad es volver al origen" [Originality is returning to the origin] has been taken to mean to return to fundamentals, to go primitive, form following function, or the return to God. Others are more complete. As an example, he spoke often of light, being concerned particularly with the angle of inclination of natural light and insisting, "Architecture is then Mediterranean, because it is harmony of light and this does not exist in the countries of the North which have an unhappy horizontal light, nor in the tropical countries where the light is vertical." He talked much of Mediterraneanism, even attributing to it the Gothic style. His

great masters were the Greeks, for whom he expressed a most uncritical enthusiasm, while always belittling the Gothic as an incompletely evolved and "industrial" architecture. He had a rather mystical belief in environment and family tradition. He ascribed his own abilities with architectural space to his descent from a long lineage of

Pedro Uhart with Salvador Dalí, who wears a piece of Gaudian decoration as a crown.

coppersmiths: "All these generations of people concerned with space give a preparation. The smith is a man who can make a volume from a flat sheet. Before he begins his task he must have visualized space." The majority of Gaudí's comments are rich and thought-provoking—he was a ready conversationalist and a born teacher. As a well-educated man he was prepared to converse with visiting intellectuals on many subjects. His remarks deserve translation and study, especially those that bear directly on the practice and theory of architecture....

With regard to his working methods, it should be emphasized that in spite of his improvising and his apparent rule-of-thumb methods, he was not a master mason, but an architect. His associates report that he maintained that dignity that Latins attach to the profession of architect, supervising rather than showing by example. He intervened seldom with his hands, the great exceptions being some of the iron forging and the sculpture that was designed for the Sagrada Familia church. Considering how adept he was with abstract forms and ordinary architectural ornament, we are unprepared for the dismal figure sculpture of the Nativity facade. His first error would seem to be his quite modern belief that the architect should control every detail, which encouraged him to try to train his own sculptors. The second was his commitment to a naturalism so severe that he employed life molds, death masks, dissections, photographs, and even simultaneous reflections from multiple mirrors in order to obtain exact copies of the original.

But it was just this conscientiousness over each detail that accounted for his outstanding contributions to the Catalan crafts revival of his day. No medium was too lowly for him to take on. He was proud to design banners for civic processions. He moved freely from ceramics to stained glass to ironwork to furniture design. His furniture, as we have seen, is basic to any understanding of Gaudí's work; as with his ironwork he tried to vitalize the ordinary nineteenth-century product by injecting a brisk effect of life and nature. Fortunately Barcelona had developed a

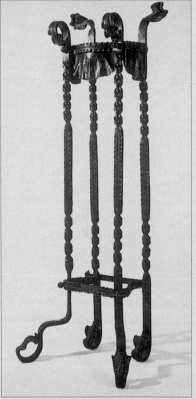

Wrought-iron jardinière from the Palau Güell (Pedro Uhart Collection).

number of first-rate shops of craftsmen who could carry out the designs of Gaudí and other Renaixença artists.

In brief summary, Gaudí's furnishings moved from his free interpretation of the medieval which we have observed in the work for Comillas to the lively insect-like constructions that he employed for the Casa Batlló or in the Colonia Güell crypt. This development is epitomized by the difference between the standing candelabrum designed for the Sagrada Familia and a small candlestick for the Casa Battló. The one is a spikey medieval thing, full of motion and space, but still insistently iron. The material of the second, not identifiable with certainty, has been molded into an image of generalized organic growth. There is a madness here that Gaudí shared with a number of Modernista designers. Some of this spirit he had developed independently well before Art Nouveau came along.... As he worked with crews of specialists on some buildings, there are variations to be noticed in style. For instance, most of the furniture for the Palacio Güell *[see pages 54–5]* was done more conservatively and the suite for the owner of the Casa Calvet *[see pages 53, 55]* was much less spirited than the sets that Gaudí designed for the business offices on the ground floor.

Catalan craftsmanship of the period is noted for extravagance of effect, and Gaudí's was no exception. Where possible, as in the Palacio Güell, he made his walls of polished marbles and rich incrustations, but for patrons of more modest circumstances such as the Teresianas he produced a polychromy with inexpensive tile and brick. The colorful tiles he designed and used were a mass-produced substitute for costly

sculptured decorations on the exterior of buildings. But it is the ironwork of the exterior, like the furniture inside, that lends his buildings a sense of animation even when they are deserted. The techniques vary in his metalwork, and the range of forms is immense; his contributions to this venerable Spanish specialty have frequently been noted.

EVALUATION

The impact of a creative personality like Gaudí's on his contemporaries and on subsequent generations makes an instructive study.

We should realize, to begin with, that Gaudí employed a quantity of architects, artists in their own right, who served him unstintingly. Of the younger of these, many are still alive today and can testify to the power of his personality and to his effectiveness as a teacher. The manner in which collaborators of the master were engulfed by his dominating personality has led later to acrimonious charges of plagiarism, much as occurred among the Oak Park associates of Frank Lloyd Wright. This broke into the open in 1928–29 in the form of a long polemic over Francisco Berenguer—whether he had been exploited by Gaudí and just what Gaudí's buildings owed to his designs. A glance at Berenguer's independently executed commissions, which are mostly distinct from Gaudí's and generally inferior, indicates that Berenguer could not have been the inventor of Gaudí's "decorative system" as was charged.

The type of exchange that may have occurred between Gaudí and other major architects of the Renaixença in their maturity has not, apparently, been studied. The isolation of his later years suggests that Gaudí was not their debtor: he was, in fact, isolated by his own volition from the Association of Architects and received much more attention from young students of architecture than from their elders. As for the practitioners of Modernismo— they operated much more under the sway of France, Germany and Vienna than of Gaudí, whose forms were the most independent of foreign influence in that epoch. The number of buildings that might be called adaptations of Gaudí's seem to be few and rather painful; none of his contemporaries, even the greatest, seem to have possessed that innate sense of unity by which Gaudí made his elements "fit"— structure, geometry and the richest decorative outbursts. To judge from their own reports, the impact of Gaudí on his co-workers was less that of specific architectural elements than that of his personality, his religious faith and his sincere belief in architecure as a way of life.

Gaudí's influence outside of Spain during his lifetime seems to have been nil. It is not clear whether the German expressionist architects were aware of his buildings, although in certain cases the resemblances are striking: e.g.,

Drawing from 1928, by Josep Maria Jujol of a shrine dedicated to the Virgin of Montserrat, which was to be built on a hill at Montferri in the province of Tarragona. Work on the project stopped in about 1930.

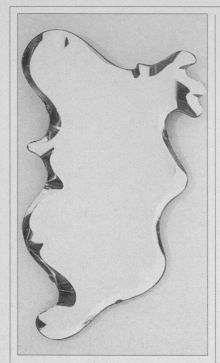

A bove: a mirror, and right: a gilt wood wall clock, both from the Casa Milá (Pedro Uhart Collection).

between the windows of Eric Mendelsohn's Einstein Tower and those of the Casa Milá mansard.

Following Gaudí's death his influence as an architect dwindled away even in Catalonia, which is what one might expect if it is true that since about 1910 his major effect has been the personal one of teacher and sage. On the occasion of his demise there was a considerable outburst of writing about him which continued for a year or so, stimulated by the exposition that marked the first anniversary of his

death and by the publication of monographs in 1928 and 1929. A survey of the literature appearing on him reveals that from then on until the late 1940s he received relatively scant attention. Reviews of the 1927 exhibition already revealed considerable disenchantment with his work at that time.

Yet there have always been some groups concerned with him. There is, after all, the cult of the Sagrada Familia. And Gaudí himself is the center of a cult. In Barcelona he is an institution: every Catalan feels strongly about him, pro or con, as an American feels about a baseball team, and even the "cons" are agreed that he was a genius. When in 1952 a scholar in Madrid dared question this, he set off an outburst from piqued Catalans that continued in the press for more than four months. Another group of interested individuals comprises the startled tourists and itinerant photographers who write feature articles about his Barcelona buildings upon their return home.

Within the arts, it was mainly the Surrealists who kept his memory alive. Salvador Dalí, his compatriot, published dramatic photographs of his buildings in 1933 which brought Gaudí to the attention of the *avant garde* during the years when most architects were unconcerned or hostile to him. An interest such as the Surrealists' in the suggestive meanings of Gaudí's forms still persists, but in recent years the craftsmen and other segments of the artistic world have become intrigued with him. It is no coincidence that the post-war interest in Gaudí here in America accompanied the rise of our own school of abstract expressionism in painting and sculpture. Here was an artist, practicing the collective, businesslike and generally unwieldy art of architecture, and doing so with that same free-wheeling, apparently anarchic individuality that characterized their own style of painting! Between them the Surrealists and the abstract expressionists accounted for a whole new taste in Gaudí-photography that emphasized the painterly or sculptural values of his forms and of his decorative details.

But today one notices that more and more *architects* and *engineers* are visiting Barcelona to look over his buildings. Attention is shifting from the surfaces, textures and forms to the dramatic structure and elusive spatial effects of Gaudí's architecture. Engineers find here their newest pet— the hyperbolic paraboloid surface; architects sense a release from the flattish rectangular shapes that they had come to think were the expression of our machine age. Had not their prophet Louis Sullivan called the Sagrada Familia church "the greatest piece of creative architecture in the last twenty-five years," saying, "It is spirit symbolized in stone!"?

The art of Antonio Gaudí is not easily reducible to the scope of a book or a photograph, even in color. More than most architecture his must be experienced in person. Works like the Park Güell or the Colonia Güell chapel are capable of being savored like an old master painting—after many visits and long contemplation, the spectator notices with delight newly discovered "passages" of structure and texture. But can such continual surprises and lasting enjoyment be attained generally

in architecture today within the conditions that contemporary technology has imposed upon our builders? That is what the engineer, architect and artist ask, and are seeking to answer for themselves there in Barcelona.

George R. Collins
Antonio Gaudí
1960

Chronology and Location of Gaudí's Principal Surviving Works

1877–82, in collaboration with Josep Fontseré. Parc de la Ciutadella, Barcelona

1883–88, Casa Vicens, Carrer de les Carolines 18–24, Barcelona

1883–85, El Capricho, Comillas

1884–87, Finca Güell, Avinguda de Pedralbes 7, Barcelona

1884–1926, Templo Expiatorio de la Sagrada Familia, Plaça Gaudí, Carrer Marina, Barcelona

1886–89, Palau Güell, Carrer Nou de la Rambla 3–5, Barcelona

1887–94 Palacio Episcopal, Astorga, León

1888–90 Colegio Teresiano, Carrer Ganduxer 41, Barcelona

1891–94, Casa Fernandez Andrès, known as Casa de los Botines, Plaza de San Marcelo, León

1898–1904, Casa Calvet, Carrer Casp 48, Barcelona

1898–1915, crypt of the church in Colonia Güell, Santa Colonna de Cervelló, Barcelona

1900–02, Torre Bellesguard, Carrer Bellesguard 16–20, Barcelona

1900–14, Park Güell, Muntanya Pelada, Barcelona

1901–02, door and gate at the Miralles property, Paseo de Manuel Girons, Barcelona

1903–14, restoration of Palma of Majorca Cathedral

1904–6, Casa Batlló, Passeig de Gracia 45, Barcelona

1906–10, Casa Milá (La Pedrera), Passeig de Gracia 92, Barcelona

1909–10, Sagrada Familia schools

Further Reading

WORKS AND EXHIBITION CATALOGS ON GAUDÍ

Bassegoda i Nonell, J. *Gaudí*, 1986

Bergós, J. *Gaudí. L'home i l'obra*, 1954, new edition, 1974

Boada, I.P. *El Pensament de Gaudí*, 1981

Casanalles, E. *Nuèva Visión de Gaudí*, 1965 (English edition, 1968)

Cirlot, J.E. *El Arte de Gaudí*, 1950

Collins, G.R. *Antonio Gaudí*, 1960

Dalisi, R. *Gaudí, mobili e oggenti*, 1979

Descharnes, R. and Prévost, C. *La Vision artistique et religieuse de Gaudí*, followed by *La Visió artistica i religiosa d'En Gaudí*, preface by Salvador Dalí, 1969

Güell, X. *Guide Gaudí. L'exaltation de Barcelone*, 1991

Lahuerta, J.-J. *Antoni Gaudí. Architecture, idéologie et politique*, 1992

Martinell, C. *Conversaciones con Gaudí*, 1952

Martinell, C. *Gaudí. Su vida, su teoria, su obra*, 1967 (English edition, 1975)

Pujols, F. *La Visió artistica i religiosa d'En Gaudí*, 1927

Ráfols, J.F., and Folguera, F. *Gaudí, el gran arquitecto español*, 1929 (new editions 1952 and 1960)

Pionniers du vingtième siècle 2. (Pioneers of the 20th century 2.) *Gaudí*, exhibition catalog, Musée des Arts Décoratifs, Paris, 1971

Antoni Gaudí (1852–1926), exhibition catalog, Barcelona, Caixa de Pensions, 1985

WORKS ON MODERNISM

Pellicer, A.C. *El Arte modernista catalán*, 1951 (new edition, 1974)

Freixa, M. *El Modernismo en España*, 1986

Loyer, F. *L'Art Nouveau en Catalogne*, 1991

Ráfols, J.F. *Modernismo y modernistas*, 1949 (new edition, 1982)

El Modernismo, exhibition catalog, Barcelona, Museu d'Art Modern, 1990–91 Le Septième Fou, Geneva, 1991.

List of Illustrations

Key: *a*=above, *b*=below, *L*=left, *r*=right, *c*=center

Front cover: The Sagrada Familia seen from the roof of the Casa Milá; photograph by Clovis Prévost. ***Spine and back cover:***

First-floor facade of the Casa Batlló; photograph by Clovis Prévost. *1* Detail of the Sagrada Familia; photograph by Clovis Prévost. *2–3* *Trencadís* at Park Güell; photograph by

Clovis Prévost. *4–5* Chimneys at Casa Milá. *6–7* Detail of a stained-glass window at Torre Bellesguard. *9* Detail of the Casa Vicens; photograph by Clovis Prévost.

10 Josep Vilaseca, triumphal arch at the entrance to the 1888 Universal Exhibition. *11* Photograph of Gaudí, c. 1878. *12* Barcelona harbor in 1888.

Index

Photograph Credits

Gallimard Archives. 42a. Archivos del Templo de la Sagrada Familia, Barcelona: 23, 80, 93a. Photo Robert Descharnes, Descharnes & Descharnes/daliphoto.com: 108. DR: 31, 37, 38–39, 51, 55b, 56, 60, 63b, 66b, 74a, 76a, 83, 92–93, 103a, 123, 125, 127, 128. Arnaud Février/Gallimard: spine, 16, 40, 58, 59, 62b, 64–65b. FMR/Listri: 55a, 73b, 119. © Fondation Le Corbusier–Adagp, Paris 2001: 103b. Instituto Amatler de Arte Hispanico/Arxiu Mas, Barcelona: 11, 14, 14–15, 22–23, 24a, 27, 52a, 52b, 70, 72a. Bernard Ladoux, Paris: 53a, 53b, 54, 71. Oronoz, Madrid: 6–7, 17, 18, 25, 28a, 28b, 29, 32, 33, 38, 41, 42–43, 44, 46, 47, 48, 49, 50, 57, 69, 79. Clovis Prévost, Paris: front and back covers, 1, 2–3, 9, 24, 30–31, 34, 35, 36, 45, 60b, 61, 62–63, 64a, 66a, 67, 74b, 76b, 77, 78, 80a, 82l, 82r, 83, 84, 84–85, 86–87, 88–89, 90, 91a, 91b, 94a, 94b, 95, 96, 97, 99, 105, 107, 111, 112–13, 114–15, 119. RMN, Paris: 22b. Roger Viollet, Paris: 10, 12, 26, 42b. Pedro Uhart, Paris: 4–5, 19, 68, 75, 116, 117, 120, 121. © Salvador Dalí–Adagp, Paris 2001: 106.

Acknowledgments

The author wishes to thank Marie-Laure Crosnier Leconte, Caroline Mathieu, Frédéric Morvan, Clovis Prévost, Anne Soto, and Pedro and Kiki Uhart.
The publisher is most particularly grateful to Clovis Prévost and Pedro Uhart for their invaluable assistance.

Philippe Thiébaut, a specialist in Art Nouveau,
is Chief Curator at the Musée d'Orsay in Paris.
He has directed a number of exhibitions:
Gallé, at the Musée du Luxembourg, Paris (1985);
Guimard, at the Musée d'Orsay, Paris (1992); *La
Lettre Art Nouveau en France* (The Art Nouveau
Style in France), at the Musée d'Orsay, Paris
(1995); *L'École de Nancy 1889–1909. Art Nouveau
et Industries d'Art* (The School of Nancy
1889–1909: Art Nouveau and Art in Industry),
at the Galerie Poirel, Nancy (1999); *Robert de
Montesquiou ou l'Art de Paraître* (Robert de
Montesquiou or the Art of Appearances), at
the Musée d'Orsay, Paris (1999); and 1900, at
the Galeries Nationales du Grand Palais, Paris
(2000). He has also published numerous articles
and essays both in France and abroad, and is the
author of various works, including *Guimard*
in the Découvertes Gallimard series.

English translation by
Translate-A-Book, Oxford, England
Typesetting: Organ Graphic, Abingdon, England

First published in the United Kingdom in 2002 by
Thames & Hudson Ltd, 181A High Holborn,
London WC1V 7QX

www.thamesandhudson.com

English translation © Harry N. Abrams, Inc.,
New York, 2002

Copyright © Gallimard 2001

British Library Cataloguing-in-Publication Data

A catalogue record for this book is available
from the British Library

ISBN 0-500-30108-5

Printed and bound in Italy
by Editoriale Lloyd, Trieste